Part Time Racer…Full Time Broke
The motorsport adventures of a club racer

ROSS P LORAM

Published by Angrygerbil Publishing

DEDICATION

This book is dedicated to every racer, mechanic, marshal and enthusiast who is as hopelessly addicted to motorsport as I am. I hope that in reading this book you realize you are not alone in your madness. Above all though it is dedicated to my Dad who has given up countless hours of time, many thousands of pounds and his own racing career to enable me to follow mine.

CONTENTS

ACKNOWLEDGMENTS

I'd like to give a massive thanks to everyone who has helped me make this, my first book, a reality. Mum and Dad have been an invaluable source of help when it came to checking the book over and jogging my memory of stories long forgotten. As the book spans the best part of three decades there is also a very long list of photographers who, not content with supplying photos for my website over the years, have now dug deep into their archives for me once more! So I'd like to say thanks to Chris and Mike Parry of Thunderpix, Graham Bunter and the Mendips Track Photographer, Martin Kingston of MK Pics, Keith Duke, Clive Marchant of GridArt, Matt Bull of RacePixels and Rafal Biniszewski of Fast & Focus for all their wonderful photos. Finally thanks to you for picking up this book, I hope you enjoy it.

1 INTRODUCTION

I'm leading as I cross the line to start lap three at Brands Hatch. As we close in on Paddock bend, I see Richard Smith pull out of my slipstream and draw alongside as we nudge towards 130mph. A voice in your head always tell you to start braking long before you do at Paddock, I ignored it as long as I thought possible only to see Richard dart in front as I stabbed at the brake pedal. 'Fair play' I briefly think to myself as he takes the lead away, but there's no way he's getting round that corner. Sure enough the rear of his car lets go and sends him straight into the ever welcoming gravel. Drivers always say they don't enjoy the misfortunes of others on the track, but secretly, in that moment when a competitor balls up, or breaks down, we all wear that same mischievous grin under our crash helmets. Sorry Richard.

The race might have been a week ago, but it's still playing through in my mind as I trudge up one of my customers driveways in the pouring rain. It's only at the weekends when I get to play at being a racing driver you see, much like many other motorsport enthusiasts the world over, our family spends all week keeping up normal jobs. Dad running a motorbike garage while I'm kept busy as a postman delivering letters to the people of the small seaside town of Dawlish. All very normal and boring. It's the weekends we live for though, which are either spent working on the race car or travelling to race meetings at Brands Hatch or Silverstone, this is what makes the day job worthwhile. It's not uncommon for me to be wondering around

Dawlish delivering the post while my mind wonders back to the last race meeting. That great move I pulled off at Paddock or wondering what changes we should make to the car before the next meeting.... 'Perhaps a bit softer on the rear end, we could get a bit more drive off the hairpin....I'm already nudging the limiter at the end of the next straight though, we'll have to alter that gearing a little...' Oh bugger it, I've just forgotten to deliver a parcel back there, mind back on the day job Loram!

2 THE EARLY DAYS

My earliest memory of motorsport is being stood in the road outside a council garage just down the road from our home. I must have been about five years old. There was a loud smash as Dad finely tuned his Banger ready for that nights meeting at Newton Abbot, our nearest track.

Banger racing was, and still is, a complete mystery to me. Why anyone would want to go out on a track knowing they're about to have a succession of serious accidents is beyond me. Yet, every Sunday on short oval tracks up and down the country you'll find these people. Maybe they're mad, maybe they have no fear, maybe they've got a screw loose, whatever it is they keep coming back for more. Some of them tell me it's very relaxing to go and have some carefree accidents, I think that's just more evidence for my screw loose theory but as long as they're happy… I think it's quite possibly more frightening to watch than to participate (not that you'll be seeing me enter a meeting to confirm this theory) as every crash looks like it could and quite possibly should have seriously injured the drivers. How there aren't more injuries and fatalities is beyond me. I've seen accidents that made the stadium fall silent as a huge smash left everyone thinking they'd just seen someone meet their end, but invariably a few seconds later you'll see the driver wriggle himself out of a window or sunroof, dust himself down and jump over the fence out of harms way, the race of course continues on.

When you look at the hi-tech world of F1 and all its safety precautions it makes the world of banger racing seem even more precarious. Your average banger driver takes to the track in an already damaged car which has been abused by several owners over the last few decades, wearing some ageing fireproof overalls and an equally used and crash tested helmet. The cars do benefit from some simple (and it would seem, fairly successful) safety modifications but it's still dangerous. And this is now, back in the late eighties when I was getting my first glimpse into motorsport things were far worse. I seem to remember Dad used to race in the same nylon overalls he wore to work during the days. Just what you want when you're trapped in a burning car, nylon overalls! Doesn't bare thinking about does it. Thankfully we're a little more sensible these days and our equipment now we race on the circuits is much closer to that found in an F1 pitlane. Three layer nomex overalls, balaclava, gloves, socks as well as other additions such as a Hans Device and a large fire eater system built into the car. The fire system seeming a sensible purchase after we've witnessed a few cars burn to the ground during our racing travels. On both occasions the driver luckily scrambling free in time.

Strangely I have no memory of Dad racing his various bangers during 1988 and '89, I was at all the meetings (the cringe worthy photos are testament to this) but I simply have no memory of the racing, possibly a sensible decision.

Dad decided mid race during the end of 1989 that he'd had enough of banger racing and parked a perfectly healthy car on the infield and gave up the formula. He'd only started on a dare at the start of the previous season and I think he'd proved his point!

With Dads banger racing days behind him it wasn't long before he was feeling the itch to be racing again. (Motorsport – difficult thing to leave alone) As a result the families MK1 Ford Escort went from fast road car to slow grasstrack car. The sensible car that my Grandad had once driven out of the Ford dealership in the mid-seventies was now, in the early nineties, painted in red white and blue, fitted with huge bubble arches to cover it's wider wheels and powered by a Fiat Twincam which resided under the bonnet – Grandad certainly did get a shock when he saw it!

Not that Dad stuck with grasstrack for long. Firstly we got entered into a very odd class where all the other cars resembled Formula Fords, needless to say the Escort towered above them and they got more than a little upset when Dad 'drove over' one of their small lightweight cars during one particular race. The second reason being that Dad suffers from very bad hayfever, (as do I, thanks for that Dad) so partaking in a sport that solely involves driving round in freshly cut fields in the middle of the summer was probably not the best idea – I expect Dad was sneezing when he drove over that car!

So, our last grasstrack meeting ended with us making a hasty retreat to the exit as people waved bits of their broken cars at us. I can't say I was too sad about it, it seemed like a bit of an odd sport to me anyway.

3 MY FIRST MOTORING EXPERIENCE…AND MY FIRST CRASH

My first experience of anything with a motor came when Dad built me a very small motorbike when I was five or six years old. It was made out of various pieces of other bikes, it was tiny, and I was absolutely thrilled with it. However, there was a problem. Dad told me I couldn't ride it until I learnt how to ride my push bike without stabilisers. Challenge accepted! After getting Dad to remove the stabilisers I wobbled off for an hour or two until I could do without them. Now, where was that motorbike!

True to his word we took my newest toy to the fields behind our house. It would be almost impossible (note the word almost) to crash here as it was just huge opens fields. In his wisdom Dad had restricted the amount of throttle that could be applied so I couldn't go too fast, unfortunately with the bike being an automatic and the field being on a gentle slope even with a small amount of throttle the bike would still get up to top speed, it would just take a long time to get there. But nobody realised this until later.

To begin with I was riding around quite well. I could stay on the thing, accelerate, brake and steer left and right. It was probably a mistake to get confident at this point as I started going faster. The only thing I can remember is going flat out down the slope of the field and then I did something really stupid, I froze. I rode straight past where I should have stopped, throttle still wide open and was rapidly approaching the edge of the field. Now what I probably should have explained earlier is that at the edge of the field there is a four foot drop and a couple foot gap before you get to the back of the garages which line the edge of the field. Sure enough I rode straight off the edge of the field, throttle still open, and straight into the wall which made up the back of the garages. I can't really remember anything after that, I was fine but Dad did say it was the happiest he'd ever been to hear a child cry. I don't recall ever riding the bike again.

4 MOVING ON UP

With my career as a mini motorbike stunt rider on hold, attention turned to Dads next move. The start of 1993 saw him return to racing at Newton Abbot, this time in the Hot Rod category. The Hot Rods are the premier class of racing on the short quarter mile ovals found across the UK and are a formula we stuck with for many years. In fact the cars we race on the circuits these days are still very similar in spec to the current short track oval Hot Rods.

Back in 1993 the most common cars were the Toyota Starlet, although the all new Peugeot 205's were quickly rising in numbers and would become the most common cars on the ovals for many years. These older Hot Rods still used the original cars shell with the addition of a roll cage, new engine, racing suspension and fat ten inch slick tyres. During the course of a meeting there are three races for each class of racing, two heats and one slightly longer final although even that is unlikely to run for much longer than five minutes. The racing is fast and close on the quarter mile ovals and although it is non-contact, it is so in the same way that the British Touring car championship is non-contact so there is plenty of nudging and rubbing for places.

It's fair to say Dads Starlet wasn't exactly state of the art but by the end of the 1993 season it had improved dramatically. That was after some work though. On its first practice outing on an empty track the performance was deemed fantastic, it wasn't until the car took to the track for race one with the other cars that it became apparent the car wasn't up to speed as it was lapped three times! Meanwhile we'd been attending some National Hot Rod meetings with another local driver, Martin Lawrence, as Dad had been working on his unusual Toyota 1000 car. The National Hot Rods were a completely different ball game, these state of the art cars compete on oval tracks all around the country and in the early nineties they were competing in a thirty round qualifying series each year leading up to the World Final in July.

The rest of the local racing during 1993 passed without incident as the racing continued on at Newton Abbot. I can close my eyes and still remember it like it was yesterday. To this day the smell of Auto Glym polish reminds me of polishing the Starlet on a Wednesday afternoon before making our way to the track. It might have been the slowest car we had but it was certainly the most polished!

We didn't know it at the time but this was to be the penultimate season at the venue as the track was demolished at the end of the 1994 season. It was a great shame as the track, although not large, had great character and the Wednesday night staging of the meetings always brought in a large crowd, far exceeding anything any of the other venues we ever visited over the years could muster. More and more often in recent years we are seeing tracks close down under pressure from local residents complaining about the noise or simply to be turned into the latest out of town shopping complex. Something needs to be done to protect the remaining tracks we have, both the circuits and ovals, before we end up with no more than a handful of tracks in the country.

Unfortunately back in '94 at Newton Abbot, reliability wasn't on our side as Dad became a spectator on the infield all too often, an incredibly frustrating feeling for any racing driver. Things began to improve through mid-season though and with the final meetings of racing at Newton Abbot quickly drawing to a close Dads starlet was getting more and more competitive.

The final meeting of the season took place on a cold and overcast night in September, it was to be a very memorable evenings racing.

Up until this point Dad had yet to win a race, he'd gotten close but not yet managed it. Following a dry first race there was a slight shower before race two and Dad broke his duck with a flag to flag win. There was better to come though as Dad won the final, holding off Martin for the duration of the race and becoming the 1994 West of England Champion. It's hard to describe to you how surprising this result was, but if you imagine Minardi reforming and winning next years F1 World Championship you might be getting close. Many said it was an outstanding tyre decision to take slicks on the damp track but in truth there was no decision – we had no wets. Still, it was a fantastic way to end the season and say goodbye to the track.

5 MY SECOND MOTORING EXPERIENCE…AND MY FIRST ROLL

Following my earlier escapades on two wheels, Dad thought I'd be safer with more. And a roof. So with that in mind a kind of buggy contraption was built. The three wheeled creation was powered by a moped engine and due to its light weight it was pretty quick off-road with only a lightweight nine year old on-board. I remember it like it was yesterday as we took the buggy to a nearby piece of waste land where people used to go with their moto-cross bikes and Radio controlled cars.

For the first few runs Dad had attached a rope to the engine, if he pulled the rope tight it would kill the engine and the car would stop. Lesson learnt from the bike. Fortunately this time I was in far more control and after a few outings I was having great fun sliding the little buggy around. I felt in complete control, a feeling which I've since learnt usually precedes a large accident, but at the time I was only nine and hadn't learnt that particular lesson!

Everything went so well during those first outings that Nan and Granddad decided they'd like to come and see their grandson in his little car, what an adorable photo opportunity for the grandparents. Of course this was the week I chose to roll the car and get stuck in it upside down. The one thing safety conscious Dad hadn't thought to include were window nets and I exploited this tiny oversight expertly as I managed to get my arm wedged under the buggy as it went over.

Due to my confidence I'd driven quite a distance from everyone but luckily they found me pretty quickly, the tell-tale plume of smoke coming out of a bush in the distance gave away my location pretty well. Despite being fine my buggy was no longer deemed a lovely thing to give a little boy, it was now a 'stupid dangerous thing' to give a little boy. Oh dear.

6 THE JOYS OF TRAVELLING

With the Newton Abbot oval now gone, Dad moved to racing at Smeatharpe in 1995. How we used to moan at travelling 'a whole hour!' to go racing, if only we knew what we had in store for us a few years down the line! Although it is very pleasant living in a holiday resort on the south coast of Devon, it gets a little depressing every time you head up the motorway for a race meeting knowing it's likely to be anywhere between a four hundred and a six hundred mile round trip. When someone asks just how far south we live, our normal answer is 'Head south until you run out of motorway, then go a little further'

By the end of 1995 Dad had sold the ageing Starlet and began work on a new spaceframed Peugeot 205 to replace it. The car we still have to this day in fact, although in truth you'd struggle to find much more than a couple foot of tubing left from the original car by this point. If you think of Triggers broom out of 'Only Fools and Horses' you'll be about there. Around this time Dad was getting plenty of practice in building race-cars as he built all new Renault Clio National Hot Rods for Irish star Keith Martin and local racer Martin Lawrence who raced in the National Hot Rods up until 1998. We attended pretty much all the National meetings during the mid to late nineties, travelling across the country as Martin gradually crept up the grid. From also ran in the Toyota 1000, to midfield with the Peugeot 205 before being a genuine contender in the last year with the Clio. I suppose the culmination of that journey was the 1998 world final in which Martin had qualified in fifth place, unfortunately getting no further than the first corner when a hit from behind turned the edge of the rear bumper inside itself before jamming on the rear wheel. Game over. Motorsport can be cruel sometimes.

I'd been watching though, what to do, what not to do. If only I could have told my ten year old self that twenty years in the future I'd be racing against these guys at some of the best circuits in the country! All very strange.

7 IT'S RACING JIM, BUT NOT AS WE KNOW IT

As the son of a short oval racing driver it would have been a fairly normal move for me to begin racing in the Ministock formula which also race on short ovals right across the UK. The formula caters for eleven to sixteen year olds and many racing drivers have started out in the Ministocks before working their way into F2's, Hotrods, or even onto a circuit series. Lots of Dads friend's sons and daughters were taking their first steps into racing in the Ministocks at the time, but the thought of racing never really entered my head. It seems immensely strange looking back now that I wasn't chomping at the bit to get into a car or a kart, but the truth was I really didn't give it a thought. I loved racing, probably more than any other twelve year old I knew in 1996, but I was just happy watching.

Still, as most kids are at that age I was being nagged to find myself a hobby, although when I clamped my eyes on the radio controlled (RC) car demonstration at the Brentwood car show in 1996, I think Mum must have been regretting her words. I was instantly hooked on the idea and nothing was going to stop me, this had after all been my dream for over fifteen seconds!

Once back from the show I began reading up on the subject in one of the many RC Magazines which are published. I had no idea how big the sport was (note I've swapped from referring to it as a hobby to a sport) but I was soon to find out. As luck would have it a new local RC club was opening just outside town the following week and we travelled up to take a look. As we drove into the pits and caught site of all the racers, hard at work preparing their cars, I knew I'd have to do this. The track looked extremely impressive, as did the sophisticated 1/10th scale touring cars which were whizzing round at unbelievable speeds. As impressive as all this was, it didn't look like the place for a beginner, both in terms of expense and skill, so the next week me and Dad travelled to a Wednesday night RC Ministock club in Paignton.

The club raced in Curledge Street school hall and what hit me first when we entered was the very distinctive smell - it turned out to be the tyre additive. The cars were smaller 1/12th scale versions and raced on a special racing carpet surface. The cars were much cheaper and more suitable for a complete beginner so we decided this is where I would start racing. Thankfully Dads friend 'Deano' helped out by building a car for me. It's hard to think looking back that both me and Dad were flummoxed by a small and simple 1/12th scale RC car when he'd just built a completely new National Hot Rod and I could assemble a complicated 1/10th scale RC car blindfolded a few years after, but back then we were definitely grateful for the help!

It was a few short weeks later when Dean rang to say my newest toy was complete and I was more thrilled with that car than any of the latest carbon and titanium RC touring cars I'd have in the years that followed. And probably more than the current full sized race car I have today!

We first run the car at an empty car park near our house and after a few hours spent getting to grips with it we attended the next Wednesday night meeting at Curledge street. I took my place on the rostrum for race one with my new car, a mini replica of Dad's Hot Rod, on the grid in front of me. I've been lucky enough to make a few of the top finals at National RC meetings since then but still the nerves didn't compare to what I felt that night. Despite this the race went well and I did fourteen laps between crashes which was very respectable for a beginner. It seems racing all my toy RC cars around our home all through my childhood had been worth it, although no doubt the skirting boards still bear the scars from my earlier 'practice sessions'.

It's fair to say I absolutely loved my new hobby and as the weeks went by I got better and better. By the time the first 'Finals night' came around a few months later I'd done well enough to be placed in the top heat with the top drivers, including Deano, Tribble, Warwick, Tony – I still remember it like it was yesterday. If I'd managed to shake my nerves during the preceding months they were back in force that night! By some miracle I took third overall by the evenings end, 'new boy upset' as I was referred to as I collected my prize, this was great...

8 DAD GETS A NEW TOY TOO

Whilst I was busy with my new hobby, work was also progressing on with Dads new Hot Rod. It had taken longer than planned to complete due to all our National Hot Rod adventures with Martin, but it was still coming together. Thankfully our friend Paul was helping out and letting us use his garage / sprayshop to store and work on the car. Meanwhile we were joined by another Paul (known as PC because it all got far too confusing) who would also be a fairly permanent fixture in the team for many years, both helping out at the garage and coming to the meetings. All help was of course very appreciated. I often hear people asking how they can get involved in motorsport and saying that they'd love to be doing what we're doing at the weekends. The simple truth is you can! Most club racers fund their own racing and do the majority of the work on their own cars. With there being so many racers in the UK (we are the global home of motorsport after all) there's bound to be a few drivers local to you, so if you really want to be involved just get to know them. Most of us are glad to have any help we can get. Now it's unrealistic to expect that you'll walk in and be running the show on day one, but start small (yes, even sweeping the floor and making the tea is a job to be done) and then build up from there. If things go well, and when you have more of an understanding, then you'll be doing the bigger jobs. Even if you do happen to be a brilliant mechanic, you can't expect to be trusted straight away. I know there are very few people I trust absolutely to work on my current circuit car, because the tiniest mistake fitting a part can suddenly be a big issue when you arrive at turn one at 130mph! But if you do love your motorsport, if you are an armchair enthusiast, then I implore you to really get involved with it, it's a wonderful adventure.

Back in the final stages of the build on Dads new car and I can't stress to you how tight a budget it was built on. Everything was begged, borrowed or made. The chassis / suspension etc was of course fully self-built, while most of the running gear had been salvaged from the Starlet. Some of the panels were also salvaged from the back of Martins garage and repaired whereas a couple were actually new, although our friends Tony and Jacqui who made the fibreglass panels for Hot Rods at the time didn't exactly charge us very much. I know you hear back of the grid F1 teams moaning about their yearly budget but they don't know what a tight budget is!

With the completion of the build in sight, Paul prepared and sprayed the panels to his usual meticulous standards while someone was roped in to do the signwriting. He wasn't paid obviously, what kind of people do you think we are? We just owed someone else a favour.

Just three days to the planned debut of the car and realisation dawned that we didn't have a trailer! No matter, one was hastily built from some steel that was found lying around. The bed of the trailer meanwhile was made from wooden boards. Their intended use had been for the table sections on powered wheelchairs and Paul had literally thousands of them lying around after someone had brought them to him to spray and then vanished never to be seen again. As they weren't being used for wheelchairs any-time soon, they began a new life as a trailer! The whole thing was thrown together and finished in hammerite. It may not have been the prettiest contraption, but it did its job for six years and many thousands of miles until we replaced it with a rather snazzy Brian James Trailer in 2004, it was even sold for £100 if memory serves me right. Bargain.

May 4th 1998 saw Dads new car debuted at a windy Smeatharpe Stadium. The car proved to be reliable but was way off the pace as it was for the remainder of the 1998 season. It was very apparent that while the old Pinto engine had given the Starlet a respectable turn of speed, it was struggling in the Peugeot. This was all due to the weight, the Peugeot coming in at getting close to 900kgs while at a guess the Starlet would barely have topped 600kgs.

Before the 1999 season the engine was rebuilt with the help of local engine guru Philspeed in the search for more performance. With the top local cars being full national spec with 220bhp to play with from their Vauxhall 16 Valve engines it still wouldn't be possible to match them, but the new engine was much closer and it was used for the first time at the Easter meeting at St.Columb in Cornwall.

With the engine being brand new, Dad and the two Pauls took the car to St.Columb the day before the meeting to run it in. As it turns out they were lucky to get there at all. On the way to St.Columb there are a number of very large hills and it was whilst coming down one of these hills that the old two wheeled trailer started to 'get a bit of a wobble on' as Dad puts it. The wobble turned into a full on fish tail as car and trailer got more and more out of shape as it went down the hill. Speaking to Paul about it, by the time they'd reached the bottom of the hill, car and trailer were using the whole width of the road, gravel on one side to gravel on the other side. Gulp. After this little adventure all concerned were pleased to spend the rest of the day simply pounding round the Cornish track, clocking up over three hundred laps in what must be one of the most boring things one has to do with a race car. Still, by the end of the day the engine was given a clean bill of health and we returned the following day for a race meeting, needless to say towing slightly slower down the hills this time.

If the new engine was given a clean bill of health the previous day, it was given a full thumbs up on race day as the Peugeot took its first win in the meeting final. Of all the wins Dad and that car have had this was certainly the most celebrated. There's nothing like a win to make it all worthwhile.

9 A RETURN TO NATIONALS

July 1999 saw us return to Ipswich for the National Hot Rod world final, two years after the last visit with Martin. We arrived with the same car Martin had raced in 1997, and many of the same people, the one major difference was that it was now our friend Sean Porter who owned and raced the Clio, after purchasing it from Martin who had surprised everyone, sold up, and moved to Spain. We had gotten some pretty bemused looks when we'd turned up for our first qualifying meeting with Sean but everyone soon got used to the idea. Sean didn't have much racing experience but he was quickly up to speed.

Most of the season was spent hovering around the edge of the top twenty in the championship, but a strong end to the season including a win at Ipswich in the penultimate qualifying round, edged Sean into joint fifteenth in the standings and with it, a place in the world final.

With the world final being 75 laps in the middle of summer it can be pretty hard on the driver. To help, we decided to fit a drink system in the car, but with this being a last minute idea it wasn't fully thought through. Red Bull was our chosen drink and a small tube went from the bottle and through the front of Sean's helmet so he could take it in. The overlooked fact was that Red Bull is fizzy, Sean informing us later that he'd spent the first two laps of the final trying not to drown as his helmet filled up with Red Bull! Ah the best laid plans.

Following that exciting start, Sean managed to bring the car home in one piece although he was clearly running out of patience when it came to being lapped by the front runners. "If that bloke waves that blue flag at me one more time I'm gonna stick it up his...." Indeed. In truth it's always difficult to be a backmarker in such a long busy race. With the track only being a quarter of a mile long, if you find yourself near the back of the grid, say twentieth to thirtieth, then by the time you've taken the start and the midfield has held themselves up for the opening few laps, the chances are the leaders will already be in your mirrors, ready to put you a lap down before you've had chance to get going. And once all the faster drivers are lapping you it's difficult to make any ground up in the race order as you're constantly being overtaken. In truth if you're starting near the back of the grid the best you can hope for are several early restarts or a wet race. There's nothing like a wet race to really shuffle the pack, to give the underdog their day. Even in F1 a good wet race throws up the most unexpected results like the Jordan 1-2 at Spa, or Dad seeming to win every time it rained. I may have still been racing radio controlled cars at the time, but I was still watching and taking it all in, which as it turns out was a good thing.

10 IT'S NOT FULL SCALE YET, BUT IT'S GETTING CLOSER

I was feeling fairly flush during the early months of 2000 after leaving my job at Nortel Networks with a pretty generous settlement. Well actually not so much 'leaving' as being made redundant but that's another story. The important thing was I was sixteen with a good few thousand pounds in my pocket, obviously it was going to get spent on some form of car or another! Using some of the money I decided to make the step-up to 1/10th scale Radio Controlled Touring cars. These were the cars I originally looked at back in 1996. They were incredibly technical and very expensive. I think I spent around £1000 on the basic set-up but of course as in any motorsport the expense will always keep coming.

It's fair to say I struggled big time at first. As opposed to the ministocks it was not enough to simply charge a set of batteries, put them in the car and race. With their four wheel drive, adjustable damping, springs rates, diffs, castor, camber etc, the cars need maintenance and serious set-up work. I had no idea how to go about this so it was of course highly helpful to have a Dad who raced real cars to teach me about corner weights and how to cure various handling problems with the car. So with a set of kitchen scales, the corner weights were set with the car sitting on the coffee table, infinitely easier than crawling around on the garage floor adjusting the full sized version! Still, it was all good practice.

Now with a reliable car that pretty much behaved itself I could begin learning how to race. Despite being little more than one foot long, they achieve speeds of over 30mph and scale speeds of well over 200mph. With 4WD and suspension as you'll find on many real race cars (just tiny) cornering speeds are also very high, it's all you can do to turn your head fast enough to keep up. Progress was slow as we raced at several local clubs during 2000 but things slowly came together over the years, still, more on that later.

11 MORE DEVELOPMENTS

Back in the realms of the full sized cars, more developments followed on Dads Peugeot and at the close of the 1999 season the car was put on a serious diet and lost close to 100kgs. An unbelievable amount, especially as I look at the lengths we go to these days to get a couple kilograms out of the car. This was mainly achieved through a new set of lighter panels. With Tony and Jacqui selling up their TJ Panels fibre glassing business we took the opportunity to purchase a set of the Peugeot moulds so we could produce our own panels. We were left wondering what on earth we had done as the first wing took ages to produce, but a little practice later and it has turned into a sound investment. Had we needed to purchase panels over the years the cost would have run into many thousands of pounds by now. That's what we have to keep telling ourselves anyway as the fibre glassing is messy work, especially the way I do it. I can only admire the people who have to work with it all day every day.

The car was certainly much friskier in its new lightweight guise and after a much improved showing in 2000, hopes were high for 2001. We still had our old Pinto under the bonnet so it wasn't the fastest car on the track but it was very consistent which kept Dads #262 machine hovering near the top end of the Autospeed Points Charts as Dad raced across the Southwest at Smeatharpe, St.Columb and St.Day.

It was disappointing to end 2001 with no wins but the 1st January 2002 saw this put right as Dad won the final at St.Day by a huge margin, such a margin in fact that he was following the drivers around at the end of the race who were fighting for second place. St.Day is an insane track. Located down in deepest Cornwall it's not really an oval. A bumpy 'straight' leads into a near hairpin right, the track then continues to bend right before tightening. It's just about flat out in a hot rod as they slide downhill through the right hander, brushing the inside kerb with the destructive steel plate fence waiting just a couple car widths to the left. The fence is possibly one of the scariest things about the venue, originally smooth it's been bent out of shape by too many bangers being launched into it over the years and now is more a sequence of parking bays as the fence has bent around the posts behind which support it. If anyone does get the tricky right hander wrong they won't simply bounce along the fence, it will be a dead stop, and it would be a complete mess. Providing you haven't met the fence though it's a short straight into the final right hander which brings you back onto the home straight. If it's a scary track to watch dry races on it is positively insane when you watch cars lapping side by side in the wet. Having said all this quite a lot of the drivers love it, I think they just like being scared stupid from time to time.

As the season progressed it was becoming clear that the old Pinto engine was now getting seriously outclassed by the newer Vauxhalls, so the white flag was waved half way through the season while a new engine was funded and built. In retrospect it was quite funny as Dad drove into the pits after one particularly annoying race where the lack of power had made it impossible to get past some of the slower cars and drove the car straight onto the trailer. "That's it! I'm not racing it again till it's got enough power, that's it!" Only there were several expletives thrown in as well but you get the idea, it was a bit of a 'toys out of the pram' situation as our friend Lee would say. It's always frustrating for a driver to lack power, especially when you can see the cornering and braking performance are plenty good enough. On an open lap the speed wasn't too bad, it was just very difficult to overtake the slower cars as although they were slower round the corners they'd rocket up the straight and be back in the way at the next corner.

So, we went back to the garage, ripped the engine and gearbox out and put the car back in its shed until we could fit the new Vauxhall engine. The plan being to get the engine complete and in the car for the start of the 2003 season. Ah we do love a good plan.

12 A TASTE OF THE BIG TIME

Our friend Karl who had come racing with us over the years had by now moved into the 'glamorous' world of F1, starting work for the now defunct Arrows Team in 2001. Working as a truckie on the test team, we'd often get phone calls from pitwalls across Europe. You knew it was Karl when you answered the phone only to hear a bunch of F1 cars scream past at full chat.

As we'd never seen F1 cars on track, Karl was kind enough to get us some tickets to a test session at Silverstone in May 2002. We travelled up to Silverstone on a cold but dry Wednesday morning, with our friend 'Dangerous' Tim, nicknamed due to his dangerous hill-climb antics in his Fireblade engined 1966 Johnny Walker Special. Upon arrival we found our way to the inner car park and caught our first glimpse of the circuit below us as we crossed over Bridge corner, the track diving downhill and hard right below us. After leaving the car we set off in the direction of the pits, not really being too sure how far our passes were supposed to get us we just kept trying our luck at the various security gates and the magic Arrows passes seemed to get us anywhere we wanted! Soon we found ourselves walking between the perfectly spaced trucks at the back of the pits. Ferrari, Williams, McLaren, Renault, everyone seemed to be present which was to be expected with the Silverstone Grand Prix only a matter of weeks away. Spotting the distinctive black and orange trucks of Arrows further down the queue we made our way towards them between the huge amounts of people who were wondering around the paddock. If there are this many people present at a test, just how many must there be at an actual grand prix? After making it to the Arrows pit area we were greeted by Karl who was surrounded by enough wheels and tyres to keep us in business for about five seasons. Oh how the other half live!

The whole arrangement was very open and we were allowed into the pits themselves as the mechanics worked on the car. Soon enough they had completed their work and the car was fired up. Naively I had not picked up any ear plugs on the way into the garage (as many of the other visitors had) but as soon as the car fired into life I began to think I should have. As the car was gently revved the noise was incredible, I thought I'd heard loud race cars before but nothing compared to this. After thirty seconds or so the engine was killed and the visitors were left to discover if they still had any hearing. I'm pleased to report that after a few moments of shouting between ourselves our hearing returned and we could talk at a more normal level.

Seeing that the car was almost ready to go back out on track we decided to head off to find a vantage point and see some of the action. After fighting our way through the ever increasingly busy pits, we settled on the inner bank of Copse. From here we could see the cars exit Copse right in front of us before they headed off into Maggotts and Becketts. This is a great sequence of corners and I've seen F1 cars go through there countless times on TV, but nothing prepares you for just how fast these cars are through this sequence of corners. They seem to defy both belief and the laws of physics....Wouldn't mind a go!

13 "IT BROKE!"

With 2002 nearing a conclusion, and still no new engine to put in our car for the start of the season, Dad was very kindly lent a car by his mate Lee Rogers for the first two meetings of the year in early January. Lee had won the Autospeed points championship with his Vauxhall powered Fiesta the previous season and was now looking for another challenge. It turned out to be Stock Rods for a short time before he moved onto the circuits with the Pickup Truck Racing Championship in which he still competes today.

So once again we ventured down to St.Day on a bitterly cold and this time soaking wet January 1st. It was very strange turning up with someone else's car, especially one we'd been racing against for the previous few years. Fortunately Dad found the car to his liking during practice, reporting that it actually felt quite similar to his own, amazing when they'd been built by different people with very different ideas. The first two races passed without much incident but that was all to change in the final. The track was becoming wetter, and at just after half race distance, Dad crash tested the Fiesta. Just before the braking area at the start of the lap the car suddenly snapped left and met the fence with such force that it tried to climb it. From our point of view on the opposite straight the entire roof was plainly visible as the car went up onto two wheels before coming to a stop on its wheels in the middle of the track. It was a big impact which the car took better than expected. It had been a long standing joke between us that their cars were much more fragile than ours and could not take a large crash. Lee had never given the car a serious impact and he later said Brian had done it on purpose just to try and prove him wrong! The cause of the crash is still open for much debate between Dad and Lee, especially when they've been to the pub. To this day Dad maintains that the car broke, Lee will inevitably respond with 'of course it broke, you drove it into the fence!' It's still amusing to steer them onto that topic now....then leave.

Either way, the car (which I neglected to say was for sale) was fairly second-hand. Happily Dad was okay after blacking out for a few moments. He came to in the car before telling the marshals he was fine and getting out. Obviously he still needed a bit of a moment though as he got out of the car and fell into the closest marshal, luckily being one of the more rounded marshals who caught him and took him off to the St.Johns ambulance. Dad always says you know it's been a good crash if you wake up in the car and wonder what's going on. Thankfully I've not had one of those yet and hopefully I won't!

With Dad okay, attention turned to the car, which wasn't too happy and with the next meeting only a few days away it didn't look like we'd have time to fix it, even if Lee was mad enough to let us borrow it again. Yet just four days later we were back again after Lee and Mike had patched up the car for the next meeting.

Fourth place in race one was followed by sixth in race two in what was turning into a steady but far from excellent meeting. It all looked over before the final though as we noticed the front left shock mount was cracked, probably caused by the crash the previous week. Displaying ingenuity (or stupidity, call it what you will) not seen in many other sections of motorsport, the car was ratchet strapped together and sent out for the final. From the start Dad was soon into the lead after slicing through the slower cars starting ahead. It looked like the win was in the bag until the front left began lowering itself until the bodywork was rubbing on the tyre. Luckily it all hung together for the win, what other way is there to thank someone for lending you a car?

With the next meeting not until March the plan was to get our new engine finished and in the car for then, but due to a lack of finances we didn't get back on track until June. When the car did re-appear it at first seemed to be not a whole lot faster than it had been previously, but after a few meetings and a few tweaks to cope with the improved power things were looking good.

14 A NEW HOME

2004 was a huge step forward in convenience at least as we finally found a garage to rent that didn't cost the earth and which we could keep for as long as required. During the years our race cars had lived at no fewer than seven homes and the constant change was starting to become annoying, expensive, and time consuming, as everything had to be packed up and moved from garage to garage. During the early years racing at Newton Abbot, both the banger and Hot Rod had been kept in a small council garage down the road from our house. Looking back it's kind of hard to see how we managed in the tiny garage with no permanent lights or electric. If ever we got really stuck for electric we'd run a huge extension lead from a friends flat opposite the garage and work from that. I can even remember Dad doing the corner weights on the piece of road outside the garage, with me and a friend of mine stood in the drivers seat to make the weight up to something like correct. Where there's a will there's a way!

After getting rid of that garage, the base of the Peugeot was built in Martins garage at his house alongside the Clio, before being moved across to Paul's garage / sprayshop where it was finished. It lived there for a year or two before the garage was flattened to make way for a huge Matalan store, so if you're ever in the Matalan store in Newton Abbot take a walk to the back left corner of the store, you'll be stood on what was our garage. Following this Paul rented a massive new garage next to a dual carriageway. Although nice, the place was far too big to last, you'd have had no problems driving an artic through the door and parking it in the corner. Needless to say the Hot Rod looked fairly small when parked in there.

A year later and another move later we found ourselves in Dawlish. Our very talented signwriter of the time, Tim, had plenty of space so we moved in there. It was no more than three months later when we were moving again, this time Sean coming to our rescue and lending us the use of one his massive barns in Okehampton. As generous as this was it now meant an hours drive each way to work on the car and all the constant moving around was beginning to take its toll so it was a great relief when we finally were able to rent a unit next to our friends garage in Exeter.

When we moved in we had little more than one end of the old barn, separated off by some sheet-board. It was just wide enough to take the trailer and twice as long. Thinking this wasn't enough room, the winter was spent not working on the race car but instead enlarging the garage. Once the sheet-board ceiling had been pulled down there was plenty of room for another floor, so as 2003 turned into 2004, a new floor was slowly built that allowed us enough room to work on the car downstairs and store everything else upstairs. Now with a permanent base attention could turn to the 2004 season.

We decided to make the most of our now competitive package and travel to some of the larger tracks for some Hot Rod open meetings in 2004. These meetings were held on national tracks such as Northampton and Birmingham and all sorts of machinery was present, from top spec £30,000 brand new nationals to ancient Starlets that had been lapping the tracks for a decade or two. This of course made the racing very exciting as there was a fairly substantial speed difference between the cars meaning lots of overtaking and lapping. It's often said that there isn't enough overtaking in modern motorsport and many blame drivers, track design or rules, but the simple fact is that as motorsport has become more competitive, everyone has closed up. Whereas ten years ago six seconds would separate the front and back of an f1 grid, the gap now might be just two or three seconds. It's the same in all motorsport and it seems obvious to me that with much more equal machinery we are going to see less overtaking.   That's what was so great about these open meetings as you watched someone overtake a much slower driver only for someone else to fly past the pair of them at the next turn.

Dad had many wins throughout 2004 at these open meetings and more at Bristol, and finally at St.Columb in what was a very memorable evening with a win and a third in the heats from a reverse grid before taking the Cornish Open in the final.   One of those rare days when everything just goes right.

15 NATIONAL RACING, ON A SMALL SCALE

It was also during 2004 I decided to make the step up and enter five rounds of the Schumacher BTCC for 1/10th scale Radio Controlled Touring cars. The National Radio Controlled racing was a huge difference to anything I'd encountered before. Arriving at a track on Saturday you were greeted by a huge bunch of factory backed racers practicing, lap after lap, hour after hour, to make sure they were ready for the following days racing.

Race day dawns and the meeting is run to the minute, even full sized circuit operators could learn a thing or two from the running of a National Radio controlled meeting. With thirteen heats of drivers each having four qualifiers and two finals, that makes for six and a half hours racing to get through in one day, so the basic running of the meeting is left to a computer. Once it is started it isn't stopped. Race one is run, there is then a one or two minute gap (whichever has been programmed) then race two starts and so on. There is a brief gap before the finals and then it's straight back into the action. It's the only way you could run so many races in such a short amount of time. If only the racing on the short ovals was run with such efficiency the sport may well attract more spectators. All too often you're waiting for the start of a race at an oval meeting and the marshals are stood there for minutes on end holding the gate open for someone who couldn't be bothered to get ready on time. After the first round of races at a national meeting everyone has gotten the idea that the race will start if they're there or not, you'd be amazed how punctual everyone is for the rest of the day!

It's fair to say I wasn't terribly competitive during those first few national events. In fact at that first cold and overcast meeting in Aldershot I qualified twentieth out of twenty in the dying modified class. I got up to fourteenth by the end of the finals but that was partly helped by the slippery conditions. The one major high point of that year was a surprising fourth place at Snetterton in boiling July.

The Snetterton RC track is located within the grounds of the full size venue where I'd be racing a few years later. This means you're racing electric RC cars all day whilst listening to howling TVR's or whatever happens to be racing on the full sized circuit that day which is slightly bizarre. It has to be said the RC track itself is excellent, very big and flowing with a large rostrum placed high up above race control giving the drivers a good view of the whole track. A large model shop is on site and camping is permitted which makes the whole weekend a lot easier as you can spend Saturday practicing and don't have to mess around getting to and from camp-sites. Also with it being in Norfolk there's a whole load of short oval tracks nearby so we often headed off to watch some Saturday night racing while we were there which made for a good weekend.

In RC racing (nationally at least) the top ten drivers after qualifying race in the 'A' Final, the eleventh to twentieth placed qualifiers race in the 'B' Final and so on, kind of like full sized Rallycross. Snetterton was the first time I'd made the 'A' Final at a national event, although admittedly the entry was barely twenty but it was still a good achievement. The final was even better as I came through from tenth on the grid to fourth overall by the end of the two legged finals. It really was an incredible day and I remember standing up on the rostrum before that first final, I looked to my left and Olly Jefferies was stood there and to my right was Luke Burley, two big names in the RC scene. I couldn't help thinking, what on earth am I doing here?!? I gave all the other drivers far too much respect in the first leg of the final. Although the racing is non-contact, it's very close and it's not uncommon to bang a few doorhandles during the finals. It was another local driver who I recall told me to 'stop giving them so much bloody room' which I duly did in the second final. With new tyres fitted the car was glued to the track and it was almost as if I wasn't driving it during the opening laps, just watching as it moved up the order into a clear third place. My enthusiasm got the better of me as I turned into a corner with the outside tyres on a slippery painted line and half spun the car, but I managed to make enough places back throughout the rest of the race to take fourth overall – a good day.

The rest of the year passed without anything particularly note-worthy, the season ending at Ashby, another highly uncompetitive outing as the long straights really showed up the deficiencies of my equipment. It certainly was the best track we'd visited yet though. In much the same way as real motorsport, too many of the modern RC tracks lack character, they're perfectly smooth, spirit level flat and they'd may as well be marked out on a car park. Fortunately Ashby wasn't one of these venues, the bumpy straight leads into a steeply banked and very bumpy hairpin which leads you onto the highly entertaining infield which rises and falls through fast sweeping bends and tight hairpins, the lap ending with a very fast chicane which requires you to precisely thread the car between the kerbing for a quick time. If you were going to compare it to any real life track it would be Brands Hatch, a future favourite track of mine.

16 NOW THAT'S A GARAGE

In October 2004 we got the chance to visit the Williams F1 headquarters as an open day for the teams friends and family. Yes you've guessed it, Karl had performed his usual trick of landing on his feet and was now working for Williams F1 after losing his job when Arrows F1 folded in 2002. Karl really could write a book on his various adventures over the years, he certainly wouldn't be lacking in content!

The first thing that strikes you about an F1 team's headquarters is the sheer size of it all. Huge building after building housing the design areas, construction departments, wind tunnels, machining areas, garages, as well as canteens and in the case of Williams at least, shops and museums. After parking the cars we entered one of the many buildings beside the team's huge transporters. With this being an open day of sorts, various entertainment had been provided as well as some blockages to stop the public getting to some of the more secret areas of the factory. First things first though we had to try out the huge Scalextrix track which had been set-up just inside the entrance, a massive four lane circuit with F1 cars. There's just something about a big Scalextrix track which turns any guy back into a six year old boy. There was much laughing from the Williams employees present as one of the Ferraris or McLarens was crashed by too eager a thumb on the throttle, followed by cheers when the Williams won.

Moving on we found a full size simulator before really getting into the bowls of the factory. Huge bright white areas with components being assembled with huge machines in the background. Some of the areas more resembled a medical facility than a workshop as we looked in through windows at the workers dressed in gowns working in impeccably clean departments. Room after room, we eventually stumbled across the race bay, a jaw dropping area where three Williams F1 cars sat, each with waist high worktops around the sides and rear of the car. Suddenly our garage looked rubbish!

The Williams museum was very impressive, the large display featuring every car Williams has ever been involved with. All the F1's cars lined up by year as well as Touring cars and GT cars. It was especially interesting to see all these F1 cars from each year, it really showed the development of the sport as you walked past each years car. Something I hadn't noticed until the museum tour was that every Williams since 1994 has carried the Senna 'S' logo as a tribute to the greatest racing driver who ever lived.

17 TEAM COLOURS

As quick as Dads Peugeot had been in 2004, its appearance could best be described as 'thoroughly raced' so at the end of the season it was stripped to a bare chassis and by October the car sat naked in our garage. We then began the mind numbingly dull process of scraping all the old paint off the chassis before applying a bright coat of orange. You really appreciate just how much tubing is in our cars when you're prepping the chassis for paint! We went away from our normal yellow base colour as we'd gotten fed up of going through the whole rebuild process only for some people to think we'd done no more than give it a very good clean. If you want to upset some people who've spent most of the winter rebuilding their race car then just say that. With the chassis now bright orange the rest of the rebuild took place with us wearing sunglasses. It always amazes me how quickly a race car goes back together and before long we had to decide on a paint job for our new panels. Managing to convince Dad away from his normal one colour paint job was a feat in itself, but now I had to come up with something to replace it so I turned to the National Hot Rod PC game. A lot of spectators use the game and it's not uncommon to see real life cars being replicated into digital form and being raced around on virtual tracks. I thought I'd use it the other way and our current paint design first appeared in a computer game before we masked it up and did the real thing!

Whilst rebuilding the car we gave serious thought to building all the brackets in to allow us to put a passenger seat in for the occasional deserted test day. Back in the mid-nineties the Hot Rod World Champion of the time, Ricky Hunn, had a passenger seat put in his car as he took a competition winner out for a drivers eye view of the Hednesford Oval in Cannock. This is a very high speed oval and Ricky wasn't hanging around, but you could still hear the woman in the passenger seat screaming above the engine note. Ultimately we ran out of time and effort so the plan was shelved but I wouldn't rule it out in the future, if only for the sheer amusement factor of scaring the bee-jesus out of some friends.

Meanwhile Dad's engine had been rebuilt in the search for more power and installed, the car being complete in time for the 2005 British Oval Longtrack Championships at Mallory Park. Despite the handling not yet being right, the new engine helped power the car to victory in the Open Hot Rod Class in what was a fabulous weekend. Mallory is always fun, but when you take a few people, have a BBQ on Saturday night, a stroll round the track and a laugh at the people attempting to sing in the bar, it's even better.

18 CLOCKING UP THE MILES

After winning my local Radio Controlled car clubs indoor championship, I was looking forward to the 2005 national Radio Controlled season. We had chosen to enter the STCC (Southern Touring Clubmans Cup) which maintained entries of between forty and fifty drivers in my class, so there'd be plenty of competition. The one puzzling element from our point of view was how they could call the championship southern, a point we felt compelled to make again after a three hundred and fifty mile journey from our southern base to Snetterton!

The main reason for entering the STCC, is it was the only championship to enforce a single tyre / wheel / insert combination. This removes a huge amount of expense as unlike full sized motorsport when it is just the tyre make and compound you have to worry about, the insert and wheel are just as important as the tyre to a Radio Controlled car. So you may well have found the optimum tyre for the conditions, but if you don't have the correct inserts in they won't work at all. It's obviously a similar adjustment to the tyre pressures on a real race car but unfortunately you can't just change inserts and use the same tyres again as they have to be glued onto the rim. Take into account the thousands of combinations and you can see that it's incredibly expensive and immensely frustrating to try and find just the right combination for any given track and conditions.

During the year we visited West London, Southend, Maritime, Snetterton, Bashley, Milton Keynes and Barham, clocking up thousands of miles in the process. We really should move to the midlands one year, we'd save a fortune on travelling costs.

The first two rounds were satisfactory. Qualifying nineteenth at both meetings meant 'B' Final positions, but things improved greatly at Maritime with twelfth overall in qualifying and the win in the 'B' Final. It's always nice to bring some silverware home. This was followed up with third in the 'B' at Snetterton, the heat and time of year making this a particularly challenging meeting as the car threatened to melt on more than one occasion during Saturday practice. The driver meanwhile was struggling with hayfever. My main concern before the final was if I could keep my eyes open for five minutes and not sneeze, I know the record sheets say I was third but I didn't see much of it! Bashley was up next and I still knocking on the 'A' Final door with twelfth in qualifying and second in the 'B' during the finals.

This second season of national RC competition was much more successful than the first. I think it takes a season to adapt to any new level of competition. Bigger grids, better drivers, huge tracks, practice days, condition changes, it all takes time and in this second year things went a lot more smoothly.

Talking of National competition, after a successful start to 2005 Dad had decided to have a bash (maybe literally) at the National Hot Rods. His first national meeting was a Saturday night event at Ipswich on the 31st July 2005. We travelled up to the track early and there was certainly a strange feeling as this time it wasn't Martin or Sean racing.

Since we'd last had any involvement with the nationals in 1999 the tyre rules had changed. No longer was the Avon A10 the control tyre, it was now a Hoosier H12. The reason for the change was financial with the Hoosiers coming in at £100 per tyre whereas the Avons had risen to £125 a piece. So just looking at the figures it seemed like a good move, although nobody seemed to take into account the quality of the product. Whereas the Avons were consistent and well known, the Hoosiers were incredibly erratic and we would certainly much rather be racing on the old Avons.

Back to Ipswich and like it or not the car was fitted with Hoosiers for the first time. Over thirty cars were booked in, the nationals had certainly gone from strength to strength, it's only a shame the organisation was the same as ever as the entire grid formation rules were changed the day before the start of the new season. Traditionally the grid was purely a reverse of the points chart with the highest scoring drivers off the back and the lowest scoring drivers off the front. The new system however was infinitely more confusing with the race one starting order being drawn at random, this grid being reversed for race two and then the final featuring the top twenty from the points chart reversed, so twentieth in the points would be on pole with the points leader starting twentieth. Anyone outside the top twenty in the points would be placed behind the top twenty on the grid, which means it was incredibly important to stay in the top twenty as if you drop to twenty-first in the points you'll find yourself last on the grid for the final, normally around thirtieth to thirty-fifth depending on the entry. Needless to say the system was complicated, although it was faintly amusing listening to people try to explain it to one another, I know I've typed that last paragraph out a few times to make it sound that simple! I'm happy to report that a much more sensible 'average score' system is used these days.

So with the grid systems worked out Dad just got out for a dry practice run before the rain came down. The car seemed good and things were going well in race one until a puncture dropped Dad back to sixteenth, just outside the points. As seemed to be the case throughout the 2005 season, the rain came down just before the start of race two, just enough to make the track slick. Unfortunately our choice of slick tyres was very wrong as we discovered the Hoosier slicks didn't work in any moisture at all whereas the Avons had always been fairly good in damp conditions. Lesson learnt but it was amusing come the race end when the dry line meant that Dads #262 car was one of the fastest on the track despite already being a lap down from the early stages. With the new grid system there was never really any hope of making up fifteen places to get into the points and those chances were certainly gone when a spin after contact with another car spelt the end of the race. Not that that was the end of our weekends racing though.

With the racing wrapped up by 11pm we packed up and set off for Milton Keynes where I was racing my Radio Controlled car the following day – our family is indeed quite mad!

There were stares of complete bewilderment and disbelief as we drove into the RC venue early next morning with a full size car in tow, but after a few explanations all was well and the car received plenty of attention throughout the day! Milton Keynes was my penultimate national meeting of the year and it turned out to be my most successful as I qualified sixth in the 'A' Final and finished seventh overall. The racing that day was fantastic, to all the people who refuse to accept RC racing as a sport I beg you to go along to a national meeting sometime and have a look, especially the higher finals. The racing is close, fast, and very exciting to watch, not unlike real touring car racing.

While my national season was reaching a close, Dads was getting into full swing as we headed to Hednesford where the first race points of the season were collected, and then back to Ipswich where Dad gained the best result of the season with second place in the first race of the night. The race was run on a damp track and the wet tyre choice was definitely correct, one of the few times we'd made the right call on tyres all season. From fourteenth on the grid to snatching second place by a couple inches on the line, it was a fantastic result and I'm sure we celebrated that result more than many of the race winners of the season. I remember wondering how people could be so blasé about winning a race, from local short oval drivers to the people who beat me week in, week out when I started racing. But once you've started winning regularly it does lose something, I know I've experienced the same thing, both in Radio Controlled racing and later on in short oval racing. I'd certainly like to experience the same problem on the circuits!

The season continued on at Ipswich and then a couple Saturday night meetings at Birmingham to finish off the racing for 2005. The Birmingham meetings were very disappointing as the car developed an irritating fondness for spinning. It was one of those all too common times in motorsport when the problem was obvious with a little hindsight. We've always said Demon Tweeks should sell hindsight by the bottle, and luck, think how much you could charge for a gallon of luck?

The problem was eventually narrowed down to the rear brake pads and was fixed over the winter break, during which time we also took the chance to fit the front of the car back on after one of the strangest incidents I've ever seen at the last Birmingham meeting. Dad's car had managed to lock panels with another car down the straight, and although tapping the brakes to release the cars seemed like a good idea at the time, it only served to rip the front panels of the Peugeot off in one big piece as they stayed attached to the other car, not ours! Front bumper with grill and front half of the wings still all attached ripped clean off and made their own way down the straight, coming to rest on the outside of the next bend. It had all happened so quickly Dad had missed it from his view point and assumed it to be just a piece of wing, imagine his surprise when he came down the straight the next lap only to see the front of his car sat in the track looking back at him! The car did look amusing, lapping the track minus its front bodywork. It did run nice and cool, even if it probably was underweight at the finish.

19 WINTER, A TIME TO BUILD THINGS FOR THE NEW SEASON

Feeling for once that we didn't have enough work to do over the winter break we bought a new transit, well not 'new' you understand, just 'new' to us. For the sum of £1000 we acquired the well used 1997 Ford Transit Hi-Cube (we're still using it to this day!) and slowly converted it into our new race bus. It's nice to have a good race bus with the amount of travelling and time spent at the track. It was for this reason we decided to make an effort with the new one. Beds, cupboards, wardrobe, comfy seats as well as TV, DVD and a Playstation to keep us amused while we're on the road or at the campsite. Well, the new van was partly for those reasons but mainly because we'd been stopped with the old van and found to be overweight on the way to Northampton a few months previously. That was a real disaster, a race meeting to be at and unable to leave the VOSA weighbridge until we'd lost 330 kilograms. As I stood with the rest of our team and watched Dad drive the now light enough Transit out of the weighbridge, I had to wonder if this happens to F1 teams, somehow I doubt it.

So as 2005 turned into 2006 we continued work on the new van as well as preparing the car for the final ten world qualifiers of the season. Currently right on the bubble and occupying the last World Final qualifying spot in twentieth in the points after the problematic Birmingham meetings, it was sure to be a tense second half of the season as we attempted to get into the World Final. We'd done it with Martin, we'd done it with Sean, but now we wanted to do it ourselves!

2006 kicked off with National meetings for Dad at Birmingham and then Ringwood before he had to throw in the towel, on the National series at least, due to a lack of budget. It was a real shame as he was still just about in the top twenty in the standings but although our car was very good for local racing or the open series, it did, at the time, lack that last little bit of performance needed for the Nationals. Unfortunately it's always that 'last little bit' of performance which is the most expensive and elusive to find. I was to find that out for myself a few years later while also experiencing the uphill struggle of competing against those with far bigger budgets. I know we're far from alone in experiencing this problem and I don't want to come across a whinger but there's nothing more frustrating to a driver than feeling that you're right at the top of your game, that your set-up is bang on and that you've wrung every last ounce of speed out of the car, only to come tenth. Especially if you think you could definitely give the winner a good fight in equal cars! Still, it's motorsport, and if you show me a driver who doesn't think he's the quickest driver on the track, I'll show you someone who's beaten before the race has even started.

20 A NEW JOB MEANS NEW TOYS

Armed with fresh funds from my new job as a postman (I've just realised how long I've had my job!) I lined up my own national assault for the summer of 2007. Along with a number of other local racers I entered the Schumacher BTCC for 1/10th Radio Controlled Touring cars.

I'd well and truly pushed the boat out and turned up at the first meeting with new everything, and it was just awful, twenty-eighth was not what I'd had in mind at all! Although I had all the right gear, I'd had no time to test it or tune at all. It was a real lesson and I'd have been much better off with my tried and tested car which I'd won the local series with. Still, not to matter, one meeting down, nine to go!

Luckily one of my fellow club racers and friends Mike Doody had the same car. He was brilliant in helping get to the bottom of the problems and at least get the car somewhere in the ballpark which would save me months of effort. I'd first seen Mike race locally a few years previous and even though he was relatively new and not yet on the pace, you could see he would be. It wasn't long before he was racing me and by the time the national series in 2007 came around he'd well and truly blown me into the weeds! I was certainly glad for his help as there are so many little tricks and tips to get these advanced little cars running quickly and Mikes never ending search for speed taught me a lot. Turns out it had been very worthwhile helping him out when he was getting up to speed, now the tables had turned and it was him dragging me towards the front!

Competing with so many local racers at the national meetings was great fun. As well as Mike and his Dad Charles, we had Wayne Belcher and his Dad Mike (very much a father/son thing this motorsport) as well as the whole Guy family and several more whose names escape me.

As the year progressed and we moved through the season, the results got better and better until I finally made the 'A' final at the seventh meeting of the year at Cotswolds. It was a day of double celebration as club mate Wayne also made his first 'A' final appearance. We sure were chuffed to lock out the back row of the grid! In a strange coincidence it is Wayne who could probably have written a similar book to the one you're reading now, as he started with local Radio Controlled racing before graduating to national competition where he broke into the top finals at the same time as me. We both dabbled in online racing before he too swapped his 1/10th scale car for a full size one, more specifically a stock rod on the same south west short ovals we raced on. He currently races Formula Ford at Castle Combe...maybe we'll meet up on circuit one day!

After making that top final at Cotswolds, I was delighted to continue on in the top finals for the final four meetings of the season. What had started out as an absolute nightmare of a season a few months earlier had turned into a great one. It was a real lesson in never giving up and what could be achieved with relentless development. Plus Mikes help obviously. If I could just find that last little edge perhaps I could be a podium contender the next season? And finally get more than the odd mention and 'back of shot' photo in all the magazines?!? Little did I know there wouldn't be a 'next season.'

21 WHY HAVE YOU WAITED THIS LONG?

In early 2008 I'd just finished an indoor radio controlled car championship, but with a lot of different classes coming into the sport I was thinking about taking the summer off and maybe coming back for the winter season. It was also at this time that Dad was starting his own motorbike business (Brian Loram Motorcycles) and taking a step back from his racing. He surprised me by offering me a go in his car, I surprised myself by saying yes!

So it was in February 2008 that I found myself sat in a racing car for the first time, at a test day, at a small oval in Cornwall. As you'll have gathered by now I'd spent pretty much my whole life around racing, so everyone (myself included) had thought that if I was going to 'have a go' I'd have done it before the age of 23. Still, better late than never.

I'll never forget that day. The only car I'd ever driven before was my 1.4 Diesel Peugeot 106 (a car slower than the speed of dark), so Dads 220bhp, 700kg racing car on its 10 inch wide slicks made quite the impression! The slightest prod at the throttle pedal resulted in a kick in the back as the car surged forward while the brakes were like nothing I could have imagined. The cornering seemed impossible, surely this shouldn't be possible?

In truth I wasn't really going that quickly but it felt like it. The sensation of speed you get when skimming along an inch above the track is huge. The smells, the noise as the engine screams and the car bottoms out over bumps....I was hooked.

I could see Dad on the infield at the entrance to the first corner. After a few runs he was visibly rubbing his hands together, always a sign that you've got his attention. Well, his car certainly had mine.

The sheer physical effort of driving the car meant that I couldn't do any more than four runs or so but that was enough. The day had gone well, I'd enjoyed myself, gone reasonably quickly for a newbie, and hadn't binned the car. Dad offered me another go at the Mendips Raceway pre-season test day. I shocked myself and said yes again.

Being a pre-season test day there were plenty of similar cars out testing this time so I'd have a real gauge of how fast (or slow) I was going. Again I only managed to complete three or four runs but they all went well and being out on track with the other cars was brilliant...even if they did all keep going past me. I felt in control although it still all seemed so fast. Once you've been racing for a while it all seems to slow down, there's more time to react and think things through. Not when you're starting out though, it's just a blur, even on a small oval.

Seeing as I'd had another day in the car with no dramas, and didn't seem to be too slow, Dad asked the question I was hoping for and dreading all at the same time. Do you want to race it?

22 GOING RACING

Mendips Raceway was by now our 'home' track. Being only an hour or so from our garage, Dad had raced, and won, there many times over the years. Everyone knew us, everyone knew the car could win.

I felt like all eyes were on me at that first meeting, and a little envious that I wasn't just some completely unknown newbie at the end of the pits so I could quietly get to grips with things. Of course, the plus side to being in my position was that I had a good car and plenty of sources of advice if I needed it. Not that I ever recall Dad sitting me down and telling me how to drive, he obviously answered all my questions but after that he just let me get on with driving it my way which I always appreciated.

Only seven cars entered that first two day meeting of the 2008 season. A poor entry. I was delighted. My reasoning that it was fewer cars for me to crash with and get in the way of. Other than being incredibly nervous I can't remember too much about the first day but it passed without any major incidents. I got lapped in all three races I think, nothing to write home about but not a bad job for a beginner...I knew I'd seen worse.

Travelling back to the track for the second day I remember thinking I could win. I also remember being surprised by thinking that. Firstly, I hadn't even finished on the lead lap yet, and secondly, the three time Hot Rod world champion and local hero Colin White would be racing. I still thought it though.....

Short oval races are usually run with the slowest drivers starting at the front of the grid and the fastest at the rear. As a newcomer therefore I would get to start at the front, something I had passed the chance of on the previous day, but we'd decided to give it a go on day two.

So, I started race one on pole for the first time and sure enough everyone passed me. But then at about half race distance I started catching a group of cars again. Suddenly I was with them....oh god, I'm going to have to overtake something! The track suddenly seemed to have shrunk in front of me but I managed to pass someone and not finish last. I'd have gone home happy then.

I had a good talk to myself before race two, it's something I always do now before any race or qualifying session. Just a run through in my head of the track, where I'll be braking, changing gear, who's around me on the grid, who to watch out for etc etc I've never spoken to any other drivers but I guess everyone goes through a similar thought process before a race, either that or I'm just a bit pedantic.

Still, I digress. Before the race I told myself I just needed to be braver on the cold tyres at the start, I was as quick as most of them by mid race when the tyres had warmed up properly. Also, I'd seen this car win here plenty of times. If Dad was starting on pole he would win, no question. Right then...

Mr.Starter climbed up to his perch above the start finish line and picked up his green flag. He held it in the air and checked that all the cars were in position before waving it to begin the race. In truth you never really saw the green flag wave. As soon as his elbow started moving you were off, and if you could be rolling a little bit at the same time all the better!

There'd be plenty of time to pick up those little tricks later on, but for now it was a decent start and I remember making an effort to throw the car at the track straight away even though it felt clumsy on its cold tyres. It's lucky I happened to have a bit of natural talent really or it could all have gone very wrong a few times during the early meetings.

A couple laps into the race I was still leading and I could see the cars behind climbing all over each other trying to get past the guy in second place. I was away and clear. Lap by lap, little by little, I was increasing the lead. I couldn't believe it. I just drove Radio controlled cars, this couldn't be right could it? Then the strangest thing happened. I'd gotten far enough away from the others that I couldn't see them in my mirrors anymore, but because they were all so bunched up I couldn't see any of them in front either. For quite a few laps it just felt like I was on my own which was a very odd feeling. The inevitable happened five laps from the end and I saw a very fast moving Colin White closing in, the very same guy I saw dominate National Hot Rods for years when I was growing up. But he'd left it too late, I knew enough to know that. Count down the laps, don't do anything silly. Four, three, two, one lap to go. Nice and gentle, you can do this. Out of the final corner, onto the power, I can see Mr.Starter with the chequered flag, he's waving it at me! I can see his smile from here as I cross under him and punch the steering wheel in sheer delight and amazement. That just happened!

I still have a video that Mum took of that race and it makes hilarious viewing as it dawns on everyone that the newbie is going to win. Better than any professional video I've ever bought since. Including my hilarious laughter as I pull back into the pits with the trophy.

To be fair I've often thought I should have stopped racing after that first weekend. Nothing I could do in the future could ever compare to the sheer shock value of that first win. It's probably the same for most people I guess. My ultimate aim has always been the British Touring Car Championship, but even if I somehow made it there one day and win my first race after passing Jason Plato and Matt Neal on the last corner, I still wouldn't be as surprised as I was on that day at Mendips in 2008.

The rest of 2008 went really well. I seemed to be getting faster at each meeting and I managed to take a hat trick of wins in my first ever wet meeting. Practice for the meeting had been dry so the first time I drove on wets in the rain was when race one started. The green flag flew, I dropped the clutch...and nothing happened. Eyes were straight on the mirror as I was sure everyone would be flying past me, but everyone else seemed to be stuck in a world of slow motion wheel-spin as well.

It seemed to take an age to get to the first corner, and amazingly I'd passed someone before I'd gotten there. The whole day was a great lesson in 'slower to go faster' as every time you tried to 'get on it' a bit you just made yourself slower. So I spent the whole day being very smooth and won all three races. In truth I did have better tyres than most of the other guys there but I don't care what anyone says, it's still an ego boost to win three races against anyone.

Spurred on with new found confidence I won the first race of the next meeting which was a good, fast, dry race. I really believed I could drive after that which is half the battle to be honest, you've got to believe in yourself.

The last meeting of the season was spent being very careful and staying out of trouble which was enough to win me the track championship. What a weird season! Dad glumly pointed out that this was the second time his car had won the local track championship with someone else driving it. He'd lent it to his friend Mike Loosemore for the final meeting a few years previously as Mikes car was damaged. Dad readily admits he was always a bit 'win it or bin it' to win the overall championship, in fact he even had the phrase 'Win some, Lose some, Wreck some' on his sunstrip one year much to my amusement. He would have won it in 2008 though if I hadn't have stolen his car.

So that was my first season racing full sized cars. I still can't believe it happened, even now.

Above – Dad with one of his early bangers. Below – Me in the red, raised at the stock car tracks!

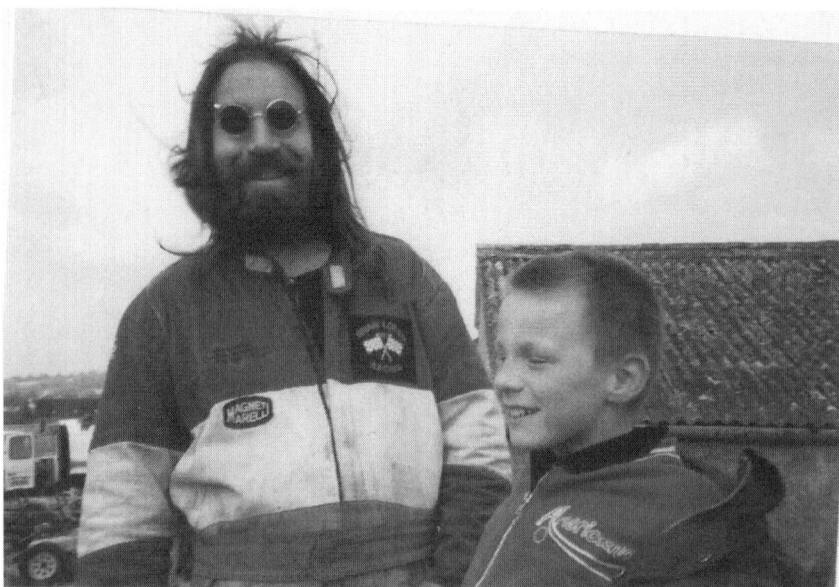

Above – Dad models some 'interesting eyewear'. Below – My
buggy…before I rolled it!

Above – Me at Newton Abbot in 1993, getting some practice in at stealing Dads car for the future! Below – Same car, new paintwork.

Above – Smeatharpe in 1995. Below – A photo that always summed
up racing to me, the rain at Hednesford in 1996.

Above – Dads new car in 1997, pictured with Pauls V8 powered hillclimb Clio. Below – Paul and Dads 205 at its first meeting.

Above – Dad in Lee's car at St.Day, shortly before his crash. Below – An accurate sunstrip.

Above and below – Freshly rebuilt and ready for action in 2005.

Above – Mum and Karl at Mallory. Below – Nationals for Dad.

Above – Spinning in the Nationals in 2005! Below – Sean and PC.

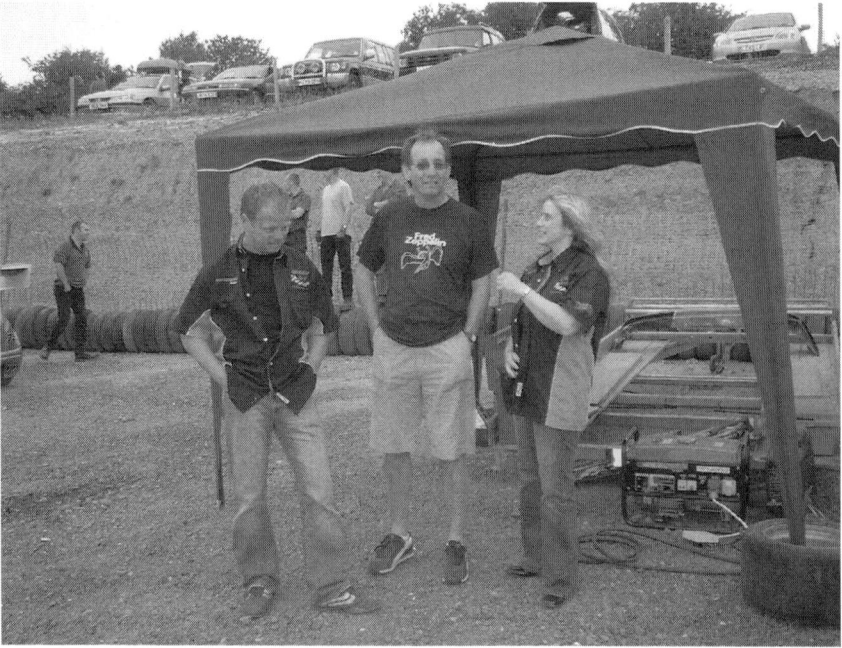

Above – Team gathering. Below – Dude, where's my car?!?

Above – Me with RC and full sized car. Below – National RC.

Above – On track in 2007 RC BTCC. Below – Dad preps the car before another run.

Above – 3rd in a local 2007 series. Below – Set-up RC style.

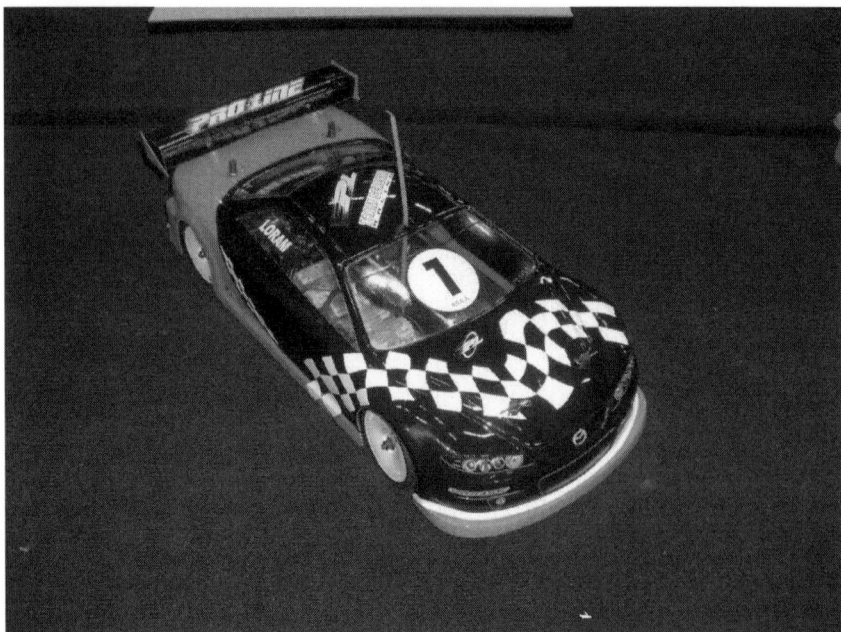

Above – My final RC car. Below – My first test in Dads car, ace!

Above – Winning at my first weekends racing, unbelievable! Below – Dad offers some advice.

Above – In the pits. Below – On track at Mendips in 2008.

Above – Me and Dad with the track championship in 2008.

Above and below – Me and the new Tigra at Mendips in 2009.

Above – Winning in 2009. Below – Dad tries the new car at Buxton.

Above – My final oval meeting. Below – Dad winning in 2010.

Above and below – Dad crash tests the Tigra.

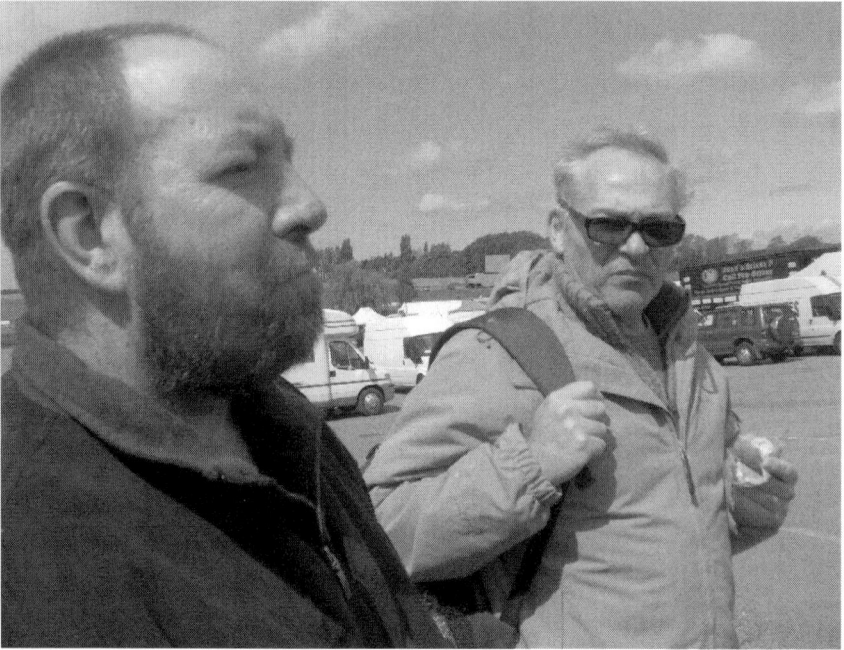

Above – Spy mission at Mallory with Dad and Dangerous Tim.

Above and below – Brands Hatch for my ARDS test in 2010.

Above – Circuit debut in 2010. Below – Problems at Brands.

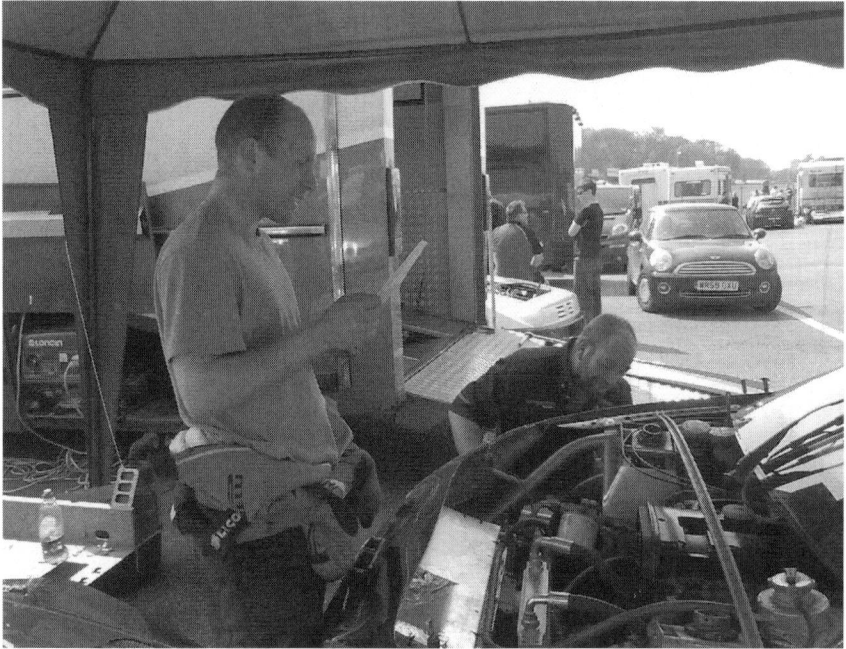

Above – Studying a timing sheet at Brands Hatch whilst Dad makes some changes.

Above – All smiles!

Above – Dad appears confused by the mess of wiring in the 206 as we stripped it at the end of the 2011 season.

Above – Nearly together! Below – Paul applies the paint.

Above – Job done! Below – Lydden Hill 2012.

Above and below – Shortly before and after Dads Mallory accident.

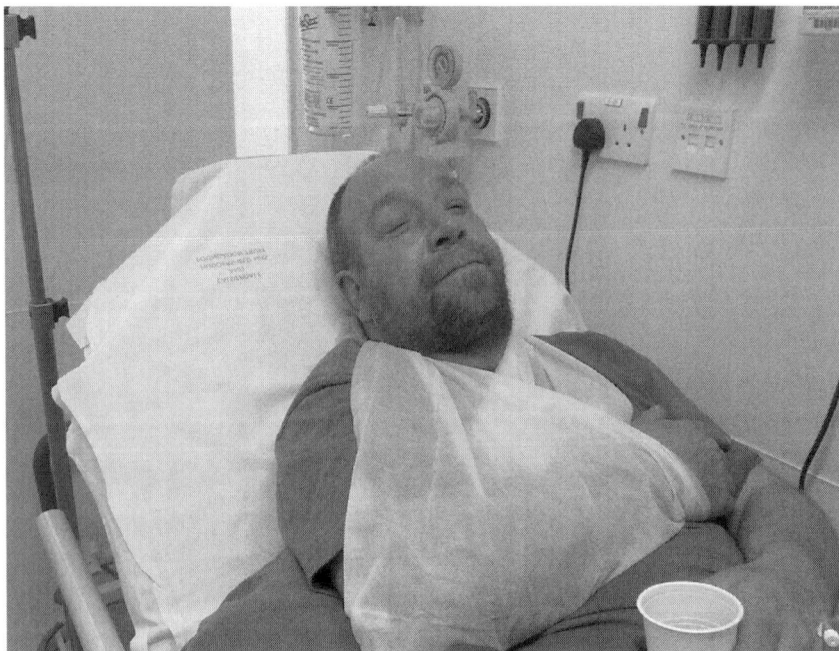

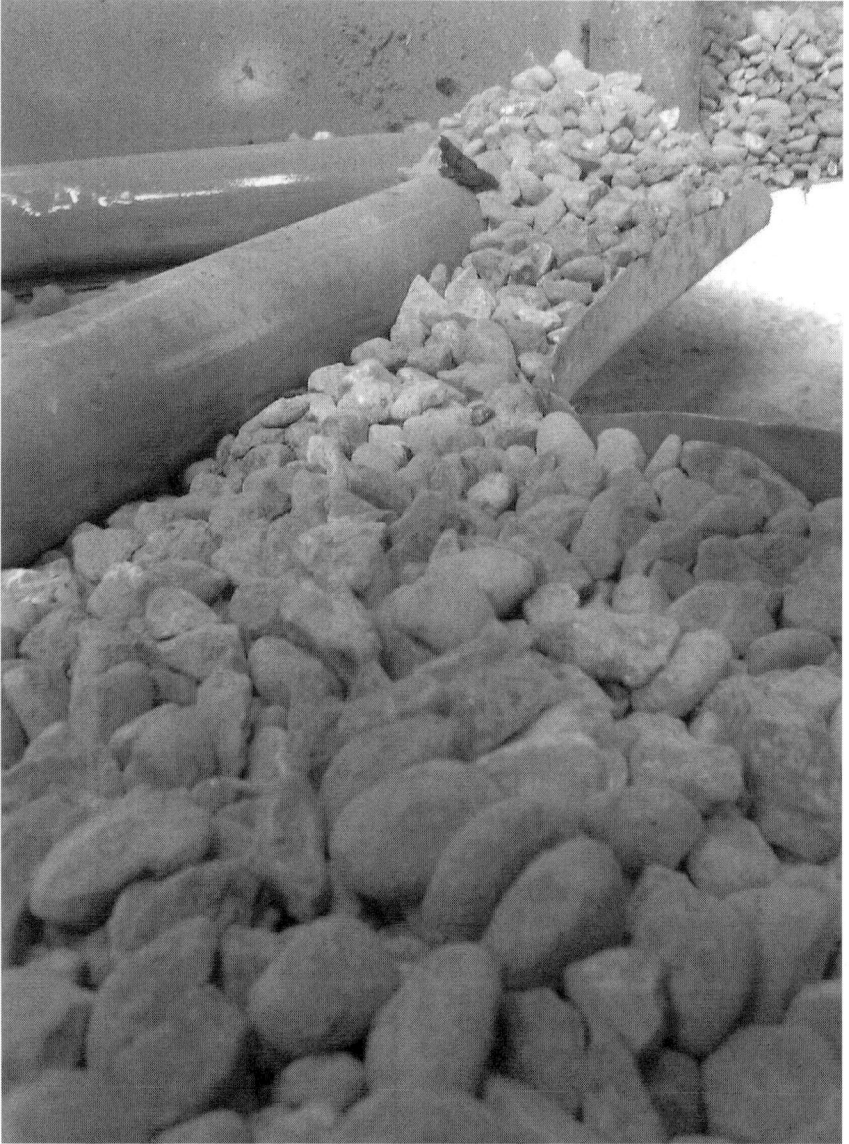

Above – That's a lot of gravel!

Above – Ready for action. Below – My favourite place.

Above – Qualifying at Brands Hatch in 2013, a good day. Below –
Leading a gaggle of cars at Lydden Hill.

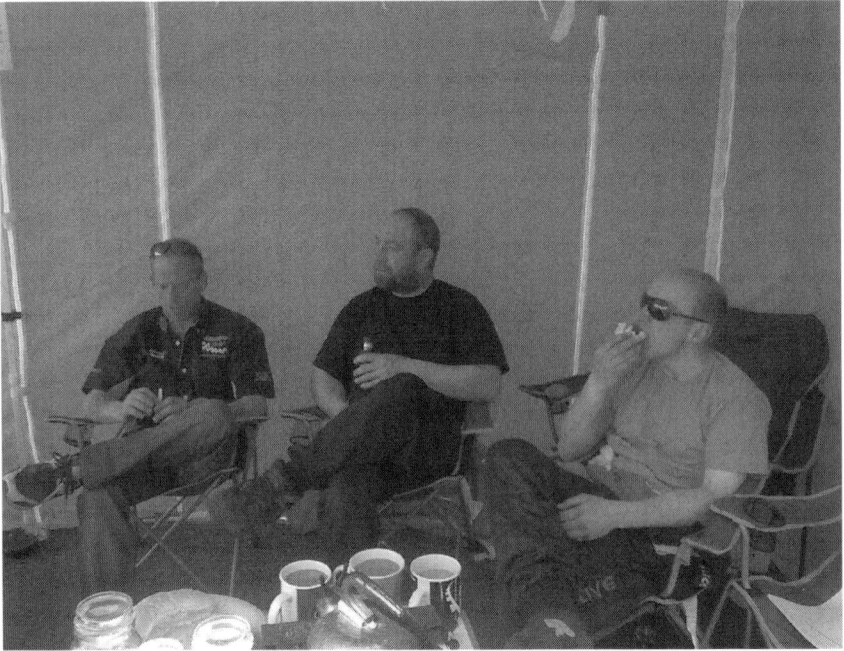

Above – Eating, a big part of racing. Below – Brands Hatch 2013.

Above – Me at Castle Combe in 2013, last meeting with the 206.

Above – Busy at Lydden. Below – A reunion of Radio Controlled racers and their Dads at Silverstone in 2013. From left to right, Charles Doody and his son Mike, Dad and me, and Wayne Belcher and his Dad Mike.

Above – Dad hard at work in the garage preparing the Tigra for its circuit debut in 2014.

Above – Does new car fit on the trailer? Below – Snetterton 2014.

Above – Snetterton pitlane. Below – Me and Dad ponder some set-up changes at Lydden Hill in 2014.

Above and below – Action from Lydden Hill in 2014.

Above – Final meeting of 2014 and probably my best ever 'save' at
Brands Hatch's notorious Paddock bend.

23 HOW DO YOU TOP THAT FOR A FIRST SEASON?

For 2009 I kept Dads car although it had gone through some changes and now sported the ever popular Vauxhall Tigra based bodykit. This was a bodykit completely designed and moulded by Dad and it was absolutely stunning. We'd spent the winter altering the chassis to accept the new panels and it was just about ready for the first meeting of the 2009 Mendips season.

I'd been pleased to add 'Fibre glassing' to my list of 'Garage Talents' over the course of the off season after I'd made some panels for the new car. It's messy, smelly work making the panels but I got the hang of it in the end and I realised I'd have to learn how to do all of the behind the scenes work eventually. We certainly couldn't afford to do what some lucky people do and just head off to a big fancy race team with a briefcase full of cash and request that the car be done and on the grid for round one! So, with that in mind I was always conscious to try and learn how to look after the car as well as how to drive it and it's a process that's still going on today. Don't tell Dad, but he does just always know more, which is handy and infuriating in equal doses!

The car looked stunning out on track at the first meeting of 2009. Unfortunately, it was awful to drive. This was the first experience I'd had of a 'bad car' and I didn't like it one bit, even if it did make me appreciate just how good and fault free it had been during my first season. The whole meeting was a struggle, lots of mid pack finishes and I remember being distinctly embarrassed at looking like such a pillock in front of friends who had come up to see us. Hmm, maybe this whole motorsport thing was actually quite difficult after all.

Back at the garage Dad worked his magic, instantly diagnosing what was wrong with the car and rectifying it. It took all of two laps in practice at the next meeting to tell that the car was completely transformed, absolutely on the button. Drivers note – learn more about car set-up.

With the car now behaving, I had one of my favourite wins later on in the day after passing journeyman Wilson Hamilton for the lead on the penultimate lap as we dived through the back markers. This was it, I really knew I could drive now. Full of confidence I took to the track for the final, and for that first half race before I spanked it off the fence it really was flying. Drivers note number two – over-confidence is a dangerous thing. Fortunately Dad builds tough cars and I managed to limp to the end in fourth place with bent suspension and a smashed brake disc and caliper. Sorry Dad!

That smashing encounter rather set the tone for the rest of the year. Lots of bursts of great speed and lots of silly little incidents. It felt more like my first season than my second! Of course you're always going to get into a few scrapes racing on such short narrow ovals, but inexperience and impatience led to a few of them. I was lucky to hang onto my track championship trophy at the end of the season and enjoy a great last meeting where I just missed out of winning the West of England Championship meeting, finishing in second. That still bugs me, Dads won that twice. I may make an oval comeback for that one at some point!

Dad jumped into the Tigra for a one off outing at Buxton at the end of 2009 where he had a good race against the car I ended up buying a few months later...small world! It was during this meeting we also discovered that me and Dad like very different things from our cars. After a season spent fiddling with the Tigra, I thought it was the absolute dogs danglies and I couldn't wait for him to try it. I'd even had to loudly protest that I was absolutely fine to travel after spending most of the previous week in hospital with a very odd and very unexplainable kidney problem. I got my way in the end but Dad was horrified when he took the car out in first practice at Buxton. "You've ruined my car, it's like a ****** spinning top" were his exact words I believe as he reached under the bonnet to make some adjustments...

24 A NEW CHALLENGE

With Dad having his car back for 2010 I bought a Peugeot 206, the very same 206 which Dad had raced against at the final meeting of 2009. After collecting it from Stoke and building an engine for it (mostly from bits found lying around the garage, no expense spared) it was all ready for the Mendips pre-season practice day. This was an all-new experience for me, driving a different car for the first time, but I remember thinking that my new / old 206 was a pretty handy weapon for the new season. Then the season started....and I just wasn't interested.

It was the strangest thing, I was driving around (in the races!) thinking ' I really can't be arsed with this'. I pottered round near the back of the field, got lapped by Dad in the final as he was on his way to the win, and I knew that was the last oval meeting I'd do. I felt like a prat but I just really wasn't interested in doing it anymore. But I had a plan.

During the end of 2009 (before I'd bought my new Hot Rod) I'd started looking at different circuit racing championships and I'd all but settled on the popular Alfa Romeo Championship. There were a lot of unknowns with the circuit racing though. I'd need a new licence which would involve a written test and an actual 'driving test' on a circuit. Then I'd need a car, some new race wear and a lot of practice to learn a load of new circuits. Lots of cash too by the sounds of it. Then the 206 came up for sale and to be honest it seemed easier to stick with what I knew. That wasn't an option now though!

So, now with a car, I began looking at the circuit championships again and there was one which fitted my car and our area of experience rather well. The Quaife Intermarque Championship. It was at the time a mix of several different classes, one of which being 'Hot Rods'. Although some work would be needed to convert the 206 to circuit specification, it was still the easiest way to 'dip the toe' into the circuit racing to see if I even liked it. Dad thought I might not like the higher top speeds on the circuits....I was almost certain I might not!

Dad continued on racing at Mendips throughout 2010 and took the final win at each of the first three meetings. It was looking good for Dad to take over the track championship until he caught himself up in a big crash at the fourth meeting which ruled him out of the running. Mum has never forgiven him for that!

Meanwhile I was busy preparing for my circuit racing debut. Firstly we travelled to Mallory Park with 'Dangerous' Tim (who was now being dangerous in a Ginetta after selling his Johnny Walker Special) to watch a round of the Quaife Intermarque Championship I was planning to enter. In an effort to see just how quick the cars were, we stood right at the end of the back straight, as close to the circuit as we could get (which is fairly close at Mallory) and boy were those cars quick! Did I really want to do this? Yes, yes I did! So we proceeded to have a good nose around the pits at all the cars, picking up tips along the way. By the end of the day I was certain we had to do this. The speeds were incredible and I loved the wide open space of the circuits. One of my biggest frustrations of oval racing was that you were constantly stuck behind car after car and on such a small oval it was quite difficult to overtake, even if you were quite a bit faster. There seemed to be much more scope for overtaking on the circuits and I was really looking forward to the chance to 'let the car off the leash' a little with all that extra room to play with!

There was of course the small issue of having no licence, so a few months after our trip to Mallory Park, I found myself at Brands

Hatch to complete my ARDS test. Having never been to Brands Hatch before I was in for a real treat, as after completing a written test (which contains questions on flags and basic dos and don'ts) I was let loose on the famous circuit in a Seat Leon for the practical part of the test. I've spoken to quite a few people since who've gone out with the instructor and been driving at 110% like they're qualifying, but in truth you really don't need to do that. In fact it's a really bad idea to. You just need to demonstrate that you're in control of the car and aware of others around you.

On the day I completed my ARDS test the circuit was also hosting a general test / track day so there were all manner of cars out on circuit with me. In a way that was a good thing as I could move over for them on the straights but then decisively move back onto the racing line for the corners. Instructors love a bit of decisiveness, test passed.

Of all the corners on the amazing circuit it was the infamous 'Paddock Bend' that gave me the biggest wide eyed moment of the day. I'd watched racing from Brands Hatch and just about every other circuit all my life. I'd seen them on TV, online, and in a multitude of racing games. Yet none of that can prepare you for the first time you arrive at Paddock. You come down the main straight, the track rises in front of you....and then disappears. It is massively steep, completely blind and absolutely awesome. And this was driving some road car with a roll cage, what on earth would it be like in my racing car? My racing car which, if it was anywhere near the front of the grid, would be lapping at the same speed as a British Touring Car? Gulp. The things I get myself into.

Despite all this I felt ten feet tall as I left Brands Hatch. Knowing I had my new licence in the bag was a big relief too as I didn't really want to spend another day and a good few hundred pounds coming all the way back to Brands Hatch to re-take it!

With the car complete and a licence in hand, my first experience driving anywhere other than the short oval at Mendips was a test day at Llandow in South Wales. Being the only car there was a bit of a relief but the day didn't go completely to plan, not least when the sump pretty much fell off and dumped oil everywhere. It was fairly lucky that the whole thing didn't catch fire. As it was, the car would just need a good clean and better fixings for the sump before my race debut at Castle Combe.

25 WELL THAT'S FAST

Castle Combe is our closest circuit, but despite this I'd never been there until we made our way to our first ever circuit meeting there in late 2010. Looking back now, the car (although reasonably tidy from the outside) was pretty unprepared and not particularly 'scrutineer friendly' with regards to the quality of bulkheads etc. Despite this the car did make it through scrutineering which was a bit of a relief and before I knew it I was getting strapped in ready to go out for qualifying and my first look at the circuit. I could see the line of cars in front of me, and ahead of them, the circuit. The only thing between me and my debut now was the sound check. I'd completely forgotten of the existence of the sound check, it's just something that isn't an issue on the short ovals. After being asked what your maximum RPM is, you are told what RPM the test will be carried out at, which is typically around three quarters of maximum.

"Max RPM?"
"8000"
"Ok, give us 6000"

So I sat in the queue cringing at the engine screaming at 6000rpm until the measurement had been taken. It was a fail. A massive fail. No amount of discussion was going to get us through this so we had to head back to the pits. Gutting.

Quick work with a deflector plate reduced the decibels slightly but it was still too high, and by this point qualifying was over anyway. Fortunately Castle Combe is about the only circuit in the country with a fully stocked onsite Motorsport parts shop – Merlin Motorsports. We assumed all circuits would have something like this, or at the very least a travelling parts van selling basic universal parts like you'd find at most oval meetings. It was only after we'd travelled round all the various circuits the following season that we realised Castle Combe was fairly unique in this respect. Lucky for us, even though it did mean spending nearly £300 on various silencers, bends and clamps. It must be said Dad does come into his own at a time like this though and before long (and without the use of a welder) he had a completely new exhaust system on the car from the manifold back.

After all the other drivers had laughed at me for actually telling the truth about my maximum RPM ("Oh no, I tell them it revs to 5000!") I had to go and complete three laps of the circuit behind the safety car before I'd be allowed to race. This was something else that was new to us. 'No qualifying = No racing' as another driver told us. This had me begging at race control, tail between legs, if there was anything I could do to be allowed to race. Hence my three laps behind the safety car!

So finally (and belatedly) I was out on circuit. The three laps passed in a blur and I didn't really learn anything. Except, our race car must be pretty quick because there I was cruising along, hardly breathing on the throttle and nearly stopping in the corners, yet the Civic Type R safety car I was following was right on the edge, proper doorhandles scraping the road kind of stuff. Hmm, maybe I should have started in those production Alfa Romeos I was looking at...

I can safely say that lining up for that first race at Castle Combe was the most nervous I've ever been about anything. Which is saying something because as a rule I just don't get nervous about racing. I've seen some people who are visibly shaking before they get in the car. They might be brilliant when they're racing, but they still get nervous as hell beforehand. Personally if every time I went racing, I felt like I did before that first race, I'd stop. I just couldn't put myself through it.

Yet sat on that grid at Castle Combe I distinctly remember thinking 'What the hell am I doing here?!?' and that I'd sooner be anywhere else in the world at that precise moment. It's not like it was even a busy race. I was of course at the back of a very mixed class field. And bricking it. Which way did the track go again? What gear should I be in where? Then the race started...and I loved it.

I didn't set the world on fire by any stretch of the imagination, but I didn't do anything silly and I kept up with some of the lower class open wheel '7' style kit cars as I learnt the circuit. I even got to overtake a couple near the end. And get lapped. Oh well, I'd still loved it. The speed was fantastic. Finally being able to let the car go and see what it could do. As it turned out it could do quite a lot and even though I was seven or eight seconds off the top pace, I'd still been topping 120mph which seems oh so much faster when you're bumping along with your backside little more than an inch from the ground. And the cornering speed is where our type of cars really shine, it was all you could do to keep your head on your shoulders. Yes, correct decision, this is what everyone should be doing!

My second and final meeting of the season would be at Brands Hatch. I remember really looking forward to getting back out on the circuit, this time in a racing car. Unfortunately it was a bad day at the office as we had a problem in qualifying and then blew the engine to pieces a few laps into the first race of the day. Once back in the pits you could see a massive hole in the side of the block where a piston had made a bid for freedom, while the undertray had caught most of the oil and various internals that had gone adrift. Sure enough a massive crowd was soon round the car. It's true what they say, if you want to gather a lot of people in the pits, just bring in a smashed or blown up car, everyone loves a look!

In truth the blown engine wasn't a massive deal as my engine was only a cheap wet sump one we'd built for Mendips at the start of the season. Most of the top end had survived (I'm nothing if not flukey) so we just built a new bottom end for the next season, this time with steel rods in place of the standard ones which had let go in the first engine. It was the first of many rather time consuming and expensive lessons we'd have to endure before we got anywhere near being competitive or reliable in a circuit championship.

26 'STUBBORN FOLKS THEM OVAL RACERS'

Following Dads big crash at Mendips in 2010 he'd missed some meetings while repairing the car, but returned for a few Open Hot Rod meetings at the end of the season where he went well. He did get involved in quite a few 'incidents' though and decided that he just didn't have the patience for racing anymore. Not on the ovals at least...perhaps Dad was going to appear on the circuits at some point?

I persevered with my steep learning curve throughout 2011. The first big lesson of the year came at the first meeting of the season at Brands Hatch, and it was, just because your car has passed scrutineering once, it doesn't mean it will pass it again!

With a rebuilt engine in the car we might have anticipated some problems out on circuit, but certainly not in the scrutineering bay! It's never good when your scrutineer starts calling other scrutineers over to look at your car. Even worse when there's five of them shaking heads and sucking air through their teeth.

"You can't race that, the roll cage is illegal"
"But it's the same as it was last year and it was fine then?"
"Then you're lucky it passed then"

Urgh! Most people would have probably gone home at this point but stock car racers are stubborn people and after a frantic hours work we rolled the car back up to scrutineering with various bits of aluminium covering dodgy bits of bulkhead, and more importantly, a massive piece of tube (which had been a breaker bar that Keith White used to get wheelnuts off his lorry) welded into the roll cage.

It's safe to say the scrutineers were surprised but they did congratulate us and pass the car. It perhaps would have been better to find out about the problem at the final meeting of 2010, that way we would have had all winter to properly rebuild the back end of the car. As it was, it was a rushed job in a few weeks before the second meeting of the season. Still, the important thing was we were racing that day. It can be really disheartening to make the effort to go to a meeting and not compete for whatever reason. As well as a weekend of time and however long you've spent preparing the car, you've also got the expense of it all. It's safe to say we race whilst spending the bare minimum, but whatever you race and however much you do yourself, you can't get away from essentials like fuel, entrance fees and tyres. With that in mind you're looking at £500 just to get to the meeting and enter. Before you even turn a wheel. Luckily our championship has a strict limit of 14 new tyres per season but even at that amount you're still knocking on for a couple thousand pounds on tyres. Big failures like engines and gearboxes will obviously cost a chunk but it's the little things that add up quickly without you really noticing.... Bleed the brakes? That'll be £20 worth of brake fluid. Change the diff? £20 of diff oil. Oh, and we could use another box of rivets, bolts, some new brake pads etc etc A wise man once said "Motorsport costs the same as it always has...everything you have" Amen.

We stuck at it for the rest of 2011, getting more and more competitive with time. I could write a book on all the little things we learnt during that first season. So many parts of the car that just would never cause an issue on a short oval, suddenly protest at the increased speeds and loads on the circuits. Aside from the engine, we had warped discs, cracked discs, cooling issues and numerous things rattling loose to name but a few. I've often thought that success is as much due to how much you want it and how stubborn you are as much as it's down to sheer talent. Of course a lottery win and an abundance of natural talent will always speed things up but we can't be greedy!

122

For the 2012 season we completely rebuilt the car. Not in a way that was ever going to gain us any massive performance, but just so that we didn't have to go through scrutineering with our fingers crossed and our excuses ready. It's safe to say if your car turns up looking like a bit of a banger, then it's going to get looked at very very closely. If it's clean and smart then you're off to a much better start. Besides, we had learnt what was to be expected during the previous year and the car was now much better prepared.

The main memory from 2012 was of a hospital visit. Not that it was for me. In a bizarre turn of events it was Dad who was rushed away from Mallory Park in an ambulance after the car fell off the jack in the pits, letting the very heavy jack handle come down and smack him on the arm. We all thought it was broken but luckily he'd got away with it, and if you're ever going to hurt yourself then a race circuit is probably the best place to do it, with the all the medical equipment and personnel on hand. It was barely no time before Dad was being looked over and given morphine....he was pretty relaxed after that.

While Dad went off to have some scans at the local hospital, I went out for the second race of the day. That was a little strange as it's the only time I've raced without Dad being present. Still, I was enjoying a good race despite some terrible understeer through the high speed corners until I got wiped out. The car wasn't massively damaged but with the lightweight panels we were running to get the car somewhere near the weight limit, it did look pretty bad as the remains of the car scraped back into the paddock. All in all not the best days racing but you can't have good days if you don't have bad days.

Dads unfortunate Mallory injury aside (which he got away with fairly lightly in the end, no broken bones, just lots of bruising) the main memory of 2012 were broken gearboxes. Most of our competitors were running the fairly bullet proof Ford 'Rocket' four speed with Quaife internals. Dog gears for those with deep pockets, synchro-mesh for those without. We'd decided that a five speed would be a much better solution. Unfortunately the five speed seemed to be a bit more fragile, especially when combined with my, shall we say, 'enthusiastic' gearchanges at the time. Poor gearbox didn't stand a chance. I've always been so desperate to be competitive that mechanical sympathy didn't really feature in my vocabulary, particularly in 2012. Fellow racer and all round unhinged lunatic Philip Young (or Mr.Cheese to give him his full name) finished every race throughout 2012 and 2013. An incredibly impressive feat. But he'd been careful with his car to do that, and I struggle with that. If there's a tenth of a second to be had, I'm having it. If it's a huge kerb or a smack into the rev limiter to accomplish it then so be it. If it breaks we'll make it stronger until it doesn't break any more. By 2013 I'd broken everything that could be broken and the car was pretty bullet proof from then on.

Still, in between the DNF's there were signs of progression, but with the championship getting ever more competitive as the years passed, it was getting harder and harder to make any impact on the front third of the grid. The only comfort we could take was from looking at the laptimes which just kept improving every time we went back to the same circuit, so we could see we were getting faster, even if the results didn't necessarily show it. That's not to say we weren't delighted that the championship was taking off though. We were now approaching the time where we would have a full grid of cars all from our class, finally a reality in 2014 with steady twenty plus cars grids from our one class. Gone would be the days of racing in amongst a bizarre mix of Caterham 7's, shopping cars, and the occasional 1000bhp Nissan Skyline. As well as being pretty dangerous with such huge speed and weight differences between the cars, it always strikes me as a bit 'amateur hour' with so many blatantly different types of car in the one race. When I see our championship on TV these days it doesn't look far removed from watching the British Touring Cars. Great close racing, similar laptimes, and all for less than a tenth of the cost. (Are you listening Alan Gow?) Whereas when we first started at the end of 2010 we had four or five very different looking classes, so we looked like a glorified track day. And you try explaining to someone that you've 'won' when you've actually finished twelfth overall. It's an on-lookers nightmare.

27 IT MIGHT BE OLD, BUT IT IS SORTED

For 2013 we welcomed a whole host of new drivers into the championship which was great and frustrating all at once. A casual glance around the paddock at the first meeting of the season saw a number of National Hot Rod world champions and all round legends, many of them in some stunning new purpose built cars. Although it was great to have them, I climbed into my trusty old 206 at that first meeting under the impression that maybe if we were going to challenge at the front of this field then perhaps we'd missed our chance. Were we getting really priced out of this?

As it turned out, no. The 206 might have been old and the odd person might have sniggered at its old fashioned struts, (as opposed to everyone else with double wishbones) but it was developed. I knew exactly what to expect from it at all times. After two full seasons we had a complete understanding and for the first time since we left the ovals I felt like I was doing a decent job on the driving front too.

I stunned myself in the first qualifying session of the year by qualifying eighth with a laptime of 50.7 seconds, a massive 1.9 second improvement from the start of the previous season. Stubborn persistence pays off in the end!

The races were great too, being able to hang with the front guys was fantastic. All that work over the previous two seasons, hours upon hours spent in the garage trying to do something clever to make up for not having a shed load of cash to throw at it. Constantly re-watching videos of old races trying to work out where I could be faster. It was finally starting to get us somewhere. There was still a long way to go, but this was a big jump forwards.

The first race of the new season might not have had the perfect ending as I slid wide on some oil on the last lap, dropping two places to seventh in the process, but as happy coincidences go it was the top eight finishers who would be reversed on the grid for race two, giving me my first front row start on a circuit. Oh dear, those nerves were back again!

There was no way I wasn't going to get into the lead of that race, however briefly, so after a bit of mid corner leaning I made it around the outside of Chris Ayling and into the lead as we exited Paddock for the first time. Check of the mirrors as we rocked up to Druids hairpin, nice and late on the brakes, turn in, late apex and back on the power down towards Graham Hill Bend. Check of the mirrors again and the angry pack of cars is swarming behind but a rattle of the kerbs and a good run through Graham Hill opens up a couple car lengths that'll see me safely into and through Surtees and Clearways. Onto the main straight and hug that white line like it's your favourite granny, no way in hell anyone is going down there. The track is blissfully empty in front of me for the first time in four years as I powered across the line to lead lap one. Well there's another first, a lap led, someone take a photo of a timing screen quick!

The end of lap two and I cross the line just in front. As we close in on Paddock I see Richard Smith pull out of my slipstream and draw alongside as we nudge towards 130mph. A voice in your head always tell you to start braking long before you do at Paddock, I ignored it as long as I thought possible only to see Richard dart in front as I stabbed at the brake pedal. 'Fair play' I briefly think to myself as he takes the lead away, but there's no way he's getting round that corner. Sure enough the rear of his car lets go and sends him straight into the ever welcoming gravel. Drivers always say they don't enjoy the misfortunes of others on the track, but secretly, in that moment when a competitor balls up, or breaks down, we all wear that same mischievous grin under our crash helmets. Sorry Richard.

As the race progressed I did of course drop back. I'd bowed to the inevitable and not wasted any time trying to fight off the guys who were always going to come through at some point anyway. Better to let them go and try to latch onto them a bit rather than try to fight them off for a lap or two and only succeed in dropping yourself back into a fight with the cars behind. Still, late in the race and I found myself in fourth place outright, only dropping behind Chris Brockhurst, and the father / son pairing of Jeff and Matt Simpson. Not too shabby. The only problem was the familiar lime green Z4 of Simon Smith was gaining, being pushed along in his fight with two of the alternative class cars in the race. Brands Hatch has a clock near the pit exit which is visible to drivers and counts down the minutes of the race remaining. I'd long hated that clock. On the days where you were reeling someone in towards the end of a race, it seemed to go at double time. On a day like today when I was being caught, it seemed to be stuck on four minutes remaining!

By the time the clock eventually relented and the chequered flag was waved I'd lost out to Simon and the two alternative class cars, but fifth in class and seventh overall after a race like that was like a victory to us. The championship was stronger than ever and we'd definitely stepped up. We'd just try and ignore where those sort of laptimes would have put us a year or two earlier!

As a happy coincidence the Brands Hatch meeting was being recorded for TV, needless to say I've watched that program a few times.

28 IN THE ZONE...OR NOT

With a positive first meeting of the season behind us, we had a new circuit to look forward to for round two – Cadwell Park. I'd been thrilled when I'd seen Cadwell on the fixture list for the first time and immediately jumped on Youtube and began watching videos of the crazy little circuit. More naturally suited to bikes than cars, the circuit is narrow but fast as it threads its way in amongst the trees, climbing and falling sharply as it does so. Upon arrival we were straight out onto the circuit to walk a lap and get a good close look. It did not disappoint and there were plenty of excited drivers in the paddock that night.

Come race day and the weather was overcast although the circuit was mostly dry for qualifying. I couldn't remember looking forward to being in the car more, but out on circuit I felt uncomfortable and didn't enjoy it in the slightest. It seemed impossible to see anything and the constant climbing, falling and banked corners made it feel like you were on a roller coaster. I'm not good on roller coasters. Consequently I felt as sick as a pig by the end of the session. I didn't want to be in this car at all.

I've always thought it strange how there are some days when you hop in the car and feel instantly 'on it' and 'in the zone' and others where it takes a little while to get comfortable. It was suggested that 'you don't have to race if you don't want to', but I couldn't really compute that so I just sat down, tried not to be sick, and got my head together for race one. I remember Dad had a similar experience once when he went out for practice and felt completely uncomfortable in the car. His solution that day had been to fit wider seat belts before he went out and won the final. It's all about confidence!

Back at Cadwell I wasn't the only one not in love with the circuit, poor Simon Smith in particular looked about as green as his car...and that's very green. Sorry Simon. That didn't stop us all being on the grid for race one though. It's amazing what a race can do and I was really starting to enjoy myself at the laps progressed. Light rain had been falling for a few laps and as a driver it's always difficult to gauge how heavy it actually is from inside the car, as even a few spots in the air can suddenly seem like much more when it's beading up the windscreen at 100mph plus. There's a reason they call it psychological rain so often, and that's all this was to me. I felt at one with the car, I was making up places and I was sure I had lots more speed left in the tank once I got past the cars in front. And then I was in a field.

Not so much 'psychological rain' as 'actual rain' then. I'd lost the rear end under braking for 'The Mountain' and had to come off the brakes and straighten up. I was then all out of options, talent and circuit, so I'd missed the corner and gone straight up the hill on the grass next to the circuit. I'd missed everything solid but had one hell of a job getting up the gentle slope from the grass back onto the circuit. Wet grass, ten inch wide slicks and a gentle slope are a bad combination. I'd tried gently pulling away, gently pulling away in second gear, going further downhill to at least get some momentum going, but no doing. In the end, first gear, frustration and about 6000rpm had me back on the black stuff but a long way off in last place.

Race two and there was no doubt about the conditions, they were awful. As we completed the rolling lap and went racing at Cadwell, visibility was absolutely zero from near the back of the grid as we headed towards the first corner. About all I could make out were a few blurry blobs of colour of the cars in front while a glance out of the side window told me we must be somewhere near turn one. Foot still down of course.

After a tentative first few laps I'd managed to pass a few cars and finally get in some clear air which meant I could see properly for the first time since the race began. Our style of cars throw up a lot of water from their wide tyres and the screens are always prone to misting. Add in their incredibly light weight and rear wheel drive and they are frisky things in the wet, especially the 206 which always lacked traction at the best of times. Mindful of all this on a difficult circuit and there seemed to be a collective sense among the remaining drivers of 'let's just drive round, finish this race, and go home' which is what we did for the most-part. I say most-part because young Lewis Smith who'd entered the championship the previous year, a day after his 16th birthday, was absolutely flying. It was clear from his first meeting that he was clearly talented, but as the years have progressed you can really see that he's something special. Not to take anything away from the other drivers in our championship, because I really believe it is a very talented bunch, but if I had a racing team, I'd want Lewis in it.

The season continued on with visits to Brands Hatch and Lydden Hill, which passed with more moderate success, before Snetterton kicked off the second half of the season in July.

29 A BREAKTHROUGH OF SORTS

I've always enjoyed Snetterton, especially since the three mile layout was introduced a few years back. It was this three mile layout we used in 2013 and I was on it in qualifying. There's not many feelings better than knowing you've got the absolute maximum out of the car and that's what I felt after qualifying with sixth place on the grid. Good days can go bad quickly in motorsport though and that was certainly the case on that day as the gearbox developed a fault on lap one of race one. Try as I might I just couldn't change gear. Having already dropped to the back of the field I realised I could just about still change gear, but only at very low RPM. Mindful of the fact that we were fifth in the championship, I carried on to the finish to try and nab a few points. Mostly in fourth gear. Incredibly frustrating, but it goes to show how you can adapt your driving to get around problems as within a few laps, and with very few gear changes, I was within five or six seconds of my normal laptimes. By the end of the race I was bored but I did have some points, and with the race one finishing positions deciding the grid for race two, I would at least start race two from fifteenth on the grid after picking up a place or two on the track and through others retirements.

Back in the pits, myself, Dad and Paul quickly had to change the gearbox and diff before race two. Always a fun job when the car is baking hot! It's a measure of how much more prepared we were getting that we even had spares to fit. It must be said that the previous year when we had broken various items like a gearbox or a diff we'd always been offered someone else's spare which was very kind. For the most part there's a real camaraderie in the paddock as everyone helps out if someone's in trouble. Of course we're all competitive and fall out from time to time, but for the most part it's a good group!

With the car fixed it was straight out for the second race. It was a case of learn it as you go with the car now on very unfamiliar gearing, but it was absolutely magic, one of those days where you're almost driving it telepathically. Just sat back and watching it, thinking 'Wow, this is good'.

Catch a car, pass it, catch the next car, pass that. Big gap in front, close it, pass. This is how it should always be! By mid-race I was up to sixth and reeling in Jeff Simpson and Daniel Smith. It had taken a little while but I'd gotten used to racing against Jeff by this point, but it had seemed immensely strange when he'd first turned up in our championship. I'd grown up watching him star in the National Hotrods for years, first in his stunning Starlet (still one of my favourite cars) before introducing the now almost universally used Vauxhall 16v engine in his Ford Fiesta, and then in later years his Volkswagen Corrado. He was now of course, like most of the field, in a Vauxhall Tigra bodied car, that was currently in my way. Come on man!

I was losing out a little on the straights but the car was mustard through the rest of the lap. I'd had a look up the inside of Daniel at Oggies the previous lap, but got on the power too eagerly on the exit and wasted the chance, but I knew that's where I had the best shot of getting past. The pair had opened up a bit of a gap to me down the pit straight on the next lap but I could carry huge speed through the fast turn one of Riches and then make up more of the gap on the brakes for the Montreal hairpin. I took as much speed as I dared through the left hander of Palmer, buzzed the kerb on the exit and headed towards the next corner of Agostini. A few car lengths in front and Daniel pulled a last of the late brakers move as he dived for the inside of Jeff at the last moment. 'I'll have some of that' I thought to myself as I went with him, coming off the corner right on Daniels rear bumper with Jeff alongside. You could have thrown a blanket over the three cars as we turned through the next left. Jeff had a big lunge down the inside of Daniel at Oggies, going straight by him, and the corner. But I'd seen it all happening and as Daniel cut back to the inside of Jeff, I'd cut to the inside of both of them. There were a bit of doorhandles and a little bit of infield involved, but I had the inside for the next right hander. I felt a slight bump in the left rear, corrected, and sped through the right hander onto the back straight. I'm still not overly sure what happened but my mirrors were empty as I continued on, now in fourth place. That's as far as I was to get though as Simon Smith had escaped up the road in third and as so often, the class acts of the field Matt Simpson and Chris Brockhurst, had checked out long ago. It's lucky they're both such likeable people or we'd all have gotten sick of them winning all the races years before!

That fourth place was like a win to us though, especially at the end of such a difficult day. It takes so much effort just to get to the meetings that you really do need the odd good result. More than anything else it's the memory of these good days that gets you through the bad days. Those days when you end up sat in a gravel trap, on the end of a tow rope, or freezing your nuts off at the garage as you struggle with whatever the latest modification or mad cap idea might be.

Following that great Snetterton meeting I was on cloud nine for a good few weeks until the next meeting at Silverstone. Whenever we visit Silverstone we use the same 'National Circuit' layout used by the British Touring Cars and most other club formula. Which is boring. I know it's 'the home of British Motorsport' and while it's great to say you've raced at the home of the British GP, it is one of the worst circuits we visit. I'm sure the full circuit is great fun but unless you're paying big bucks to race you're unlikely to ever see it. Instead you'll invariably be stuck on the National layout. A couple of long straights with a corner or two at each end. Take your packed lunch, it's a long old way. Unfortunately things are as bad off circuit as on. Unless it's a 'big meeting' the organisers don't seem terribly interested in having you there. All the most fantastic facilities on offer in the UK, all closed and fenced off in a featureless landscape. We were thrilled when it got cancelled from our 2014 fixture list, give us a Brands Hatch or a Donington Park any day.

Despite this we were of course present and giving it everything on that day at Silverstone. Big long straights aren't our strong suit, and looking back at the videos I wasn't helping matters by catching the rev limiter on quite a few occasions, but I was giving it everything and spent pretty much the whole day fending off faster cars. Defending a position on a short oval is easy. Stick it to the inside line, make sure you don't run wide (even if you're being 'assisted' into the corners from behind) and make the other guy go the long way round the outside. If you're feeling naughty a bit of mid corner leaning works wonders too. On a circuit it's much more difficult. Constant changes of direction, a much wider piece of tarmac and big braking zones make defending a position a bit of an art form. Just look at Jason Plato in the British Touring Cars for countless examples of stubborn defensive driving. You've really got to keep your head, not get flustered, and if you do get passed, try and make a move back straight away. On that day at Silverstone I think I did all of that reasonably successfully which pleased me, it felt like I'd figured out the last big gaping hole in my driving. It just all wanted a bit of a polish now!

My final meeting of 2013 came at Castle Combe, one of our nearest circuits at a mere 120 miles and scene of my first circuit meeting at the end of 2010. Three years on I was eager to have another crack at the fast and bumpy circuit. We had unfinished business.

Qualifying went well and I thought I'd gotten pretty much everything out of the car, straight lining the chicanes on the way to a 1:13.02 that put me seventh on the grid. The races weren't to go well though as I had a seatbelt come undone in race one and a brake problem in race two. It's always the way, we'd had near perfect reliability all season but with this being a local meeting and lots of friends and former competitors present, you always have problems. People coming to watch is always the kiss of death on any event!

I left Castle Combe pretty frustrated. I thought I was a pretty quick driver by this point, probably not the fastest but certainly capable of making podiums if we were all in equal cars. What really began to gnaw away at me was the fact that I'd have the beating of someone all season, and then maybe just once or twice a year they'd click with a certain circuit, or maybe their car, and then they'd be up at the front. I felt like I was always near the maximum, but that happened to be about sixth in what I was driving.

The 206 had been for sale for a few months by this point as we were planning on rebuilding Dads Tigra for me to race in 2014. Dad had decided that he had no wish to crash at 130mph so I'd be the one to introduce our venerable car to the circuits. Despite this I'd been planning on completing the season in the 206 and selling it after, but after Castle Combe I felt I'd had enough. I needed to move forward so we skipped the final meeting of the season at Brands Hatch, choosing to instead spend the time and the money on the Tigra rebuild. As it turns out that was probably the best decision we made all year.

Not being at a meeting is a very strange feeling. I was absent-mindedly delivering the post whilst thinking, 'I should be going through scrutineering now' and then a few hours later I climbed into my beat up old work van and thought 'I should be getting in the race car now!' Little did we know that the final meeting of 2013 was to be the most dramatic of the year, seeing a huge crash in the reverse grid second race. As good as the reverse grid races are at giving the more mid-grid drivers a chance to shine, they do increase the chances of accidents with the faster drivers trying to come through. Often past drivers who are in turn trying to pass those in front of them. It's easy to see why reverse grid races throw up their share of drama and that was certainly the case at Brands Hatch.

A tangle near the front on lap one caused a crash behind with Jeff Simpson crashing heavily into the spinning Chris Ayling. As if that wasn't bad enough Jeff then took a very heavy hit from behind as Richard Smith had nowhere to go. It was a very nasty crash and one that ended Jeffs racing career, although in truth it's lucky that's all he lost that day. You particularly had to feel for Jeffs son Matt and

Richards son Lewis, both of whom were competing in the same race that day, not a pleasant experience.

Although you can't avoid seeing big motorsport crashes on TV, in print, or on Youtube, it's very different to see one involving the people you race with week in and week out. It brings home that this hobby of ours is still a dangerous one, even with all the recent improvements, and that we should always treat it with respect. I'd be lying if I said our current Tigra, which we were building at the time of the accident, didn't gain a few extra tubes in the weeks after Jeff and Richards accident.

30 THERE'S NEVER ENOUGH TIME

The end of any race season only means one thing, more available time to prepare for the next one! As 2013 turned into 2014, work continued on with the Tigra. Despite being a complete car at the end of the 2010 season, it was a bare chassis sat in the corner of the garage by mid-2013, prompting the much asked question, "Exactly where did it all go?" I've long thought that race cars don't really like being in one piece. If you have eight race meetings per year, then the chances are the car will only be in one piece for eight weekends per year. As I type this for instance I know the car is up on its blocks missing its wheels, diff, halfshafts, diffuser and various panels. There's also a list of changes on the whiteboard, all to be made before the next outing. I have no doubt it will be ready in time, but not before the day we're due to leave. It's kind of an unwritten rule that the car cannot be 100% ready until the day we're due to leave.

Back in the early months of 2014 and the Tigra was very much still in its 'dry build' phase. This is where you build the car up for the first time before any of it is painted. Progress at this point is painfully slow as everything is being worked out and mounted. Just when you think something is complete, chances are there's something you've forgotten and the whole process will start again! Although I'd improved my mechanical knowledge since starting racing, the construction of a new car from scratch is still very much a 'Dad area' as I call it. He just sits down with some lengths of tube, a grinder and a welder, and builds a chassis. Not content with that he'll make all the suspension, build the engine and design the panels. Don't tell him but he's very clever. I think it still bugs Dad that one of his cars never won the National Hot Rod World Championship on the short ovals. Martin was beginning to challenge before he sold-up and moved to Spain, and Keith Martin won everything but the World Final in the Clio Dad built for him. I don't want to sound big headed but I think I'd have had as good a chance as anyone if I'd gone into Nationals instead of the circuits. With it all coming down to one race instead of a championship series there is always going to be an element of luck involved in the outcome but I think I could have been in with a shout after a couple seasons. Mum still protests that we should be doing National Hotrods and my argument that we've ended up racing most of the top National drivers on the circuits anyway doesn't seem to hold much weight with her!

By February, the 2014 back-up plan (or 206 as it was known) was no longer an option as somebody had bought it. It was incredibly odd to see the car go and to have an empty space in the garage. On the plus side it gave us a bit more room and some money to finish the Tigra! By this point we were really up against it time wise and it was a massive relief to finally be able to spray the chassis. Now we could begin assembling the car, hopefully in time for the start of the season.

Dad had long been doubting that the car would be ready in time but I was sure it would be. So sure I'd not only entered the first meeting but also booked in for testing the day before. That was probably the first mistake of the season. We threw everything at the car in the month or two leading up to that first meeting but it was stubbornly resisting completion by the narrowest of margins. While it is great being able to do everything 'in-house' (or 'in-shed' more accurately) it is incredibly time consuming as pretty much every part on our car is hand built. And that takes time, time we didn't have. As ever Paul was great, spraying the panels and helping out on the car as much as possible, but aside from him it was only me and Dad, and at the end of the day I'm a bloody postman, what do I know!

As we entered the week of the first meeting, tempers were short, the garage was a bomb site, the car was in bits and everyone hated it.

Motorsport folks, it's ace. The day before we were due to leave and we'd been at it all day. Frustrating job after frustrating job came and went, so did the daylight. By midnight we'd got the car on the scales and were rapidly throwing a set-up at it, surely this won't end well. A loud crunch followed as the car rolled off the scales and beached itself on some breeze blocks. The quick lift jack had gone straight through the rear undertray. Nearly 1am. We're due out on circuit in twelve hours for testing. The garage door is shut, let's just go home.

31 AN UNLIKELY DEBUT

We did finally make it to Brands Hatch for that first meeting. We missed testing having spent all day finishing off the car, but it was a miracle we were there at all. With hindsight it would have been more sensible to have missed the first meeting or two, instead spending a bit more time finishing off the car before completing a few test days to iron out the inevitable problems you'll always have with a new car. But we've never been that sensible, so the first time our new car turned a wheel was in qualifying, not recommended!

Heading out on circuit in that first session was like a voyage into the unknown. The main priority was to keep an eye on the gauges and make sure everything was running well, can't forget the engine has been rebuilt too! After that it was a case of bedding the brake pads and tyres in, staying out of everyones way and trying to figure out what the new car was like. Who says racing drivers can't multi-task! After a mid-session red flag it was back out on circuit for a frantic final few minutes where I'd decided it was time for a hot lap. The first seven or eight seconds of that lap were spot on, then there was rather too much gravel involved. The turn into Paddock was okay but it seemed the Tigra had rather more mid-corner understeer than the 206, and then rather more traction which I discovered as I unsuccessfully tried to kick the back end out but only succeeded in powering myself into the gravel trap. What a prat.

It's amazing how quickly a beautiful, gleaming race car can transform into something that looks like it's contested a round of the world rally championship. Back in the pits and we began shovelling the gravel out (it really does get everywhere) while Dad set to work with some aluminium, rivets and tank tape to recreate the corner of bumper that was still somewhere in the Brands Hatch gravel trap.

Before we knew it we were back out for race one where I was pleased to be able to at least finish. Of course I did have a massive list of 'things to fix' by the time the chequered flag fell, the steering was far too heavy, the brakes were frightening and the front end was awful. On the bright side it was only one second off our 206 laptimes, so just how fast would it be when it was right?

Many changes were made for race two but unfortunately the race ended at turn one as I got whacked into the gravel. I'd raced at Brands for three years without going into that gravel and I'd ended up parked in there twice in one day! After all the hours spent getting the car ready over the past few months, it was a weary team that shoved the battle-scared Tigra onto the trailer and headed back down the motorway towards home. Not the best start but it would get better, needless to say a list was made, progress was made.

32 IMPROVING ALL THE TIME

The second meeting of the season was at Rockingham. I've always enjoyed driving there and we turned up having completed out 'post-Brands list'. As a result the car was a definite improvement, not good but better. This combined with a less than full grid and a few DNF's in the second race had me running in a clear third position. But I knew it wasn't going to last. Spots of water had begun to appear on the windscreen, and I couldn't even kid myself into believing it was rain under the clear blue skies that day. With the water temperature still okay I crossed fingers and carried on. A few laps later and with the problem getting worse I had the screen misting up but was pressing on regardless. In truth, with the wipers and demister fan going my laps were numbered and I was forced to call it a day shortly after and park up the car. I knew it was a bit of an inherited position but after all the work we'd put in we deserved that result. I could barely bring myself to watch as the others flew past my stricken car.

The cause of the problem turned out to be the fan which had been gently pressed into the radiator by the ducting behind it. Over time the fan had then worn a tiny hole in the radiator causing the leak. So often it's these tiny little problems than can end up costing you a result. In a way they're more annoying than the big problems, although they are at least cheaper to fix!

Another meeting down, another list on the wall. Meeting by meeting the car was starting to come together. The next meeting at Brands was another step forwards as I was embroiled in a midfield scramble for the whole race, always good fun. List up, list done, next meeting.

It's incredible how quickly the year passes when you're involved in motorsport. Typically we have around a month between our meetings, which at first sounds like lots of time, but invariably you end up rushing to be ready. For instance, by the time we travel back from a meeting, unload the car and get home, it's usually the very early hours of Monday morning. Just enough time to grab a few hours sleep before heading out the door to work where you'll end up recapping the weekend a few times while trying to explain that just because you haven't won it doesn't mean you were rubbish and that you probably would have won if you weren't doing such a competitive championship that you can't really afford to do. After dragging your feet at work you'll be glad to get home and put your feet up. With work for the rest of the week and the garage a fifty mile round trip away you'll be lucky to get chance to have a look at the car until the following Sunday. On the bright side there's plenty of jobs to do at home. The website will want updating and there'll be videos to watch from the previous weekend, which is great fun or depressing based on the result. Then you'll need to enter the next meeting and of course figure out what needs doing to the car before its next outing.

All of a sudden a week's gone already and the car hasn't been looked at yet! Normally there will be some sort of 'issue' to investigate or problem to fix. The diff and the set-up might want changing. The tyres will want sorting for next time and for some reason the car will always come back jammed full of stones and grass so it'll need a good clear out and clean. Don't forget to spanner check too, don't want anything falling off do we? There'll be parts and supplies to get too, you're always running out of something....when was that meeting again?

Our next outing would be at Lydden Hill. We'd raced there a few times over the years but it had never been my favourite venue. I like fast corners, give me a Thruxton, Castle Combe or Donington Park any day. I love the feeling as the car just glides its way through the apex on the exciting side of 100mph. Real finger-tip stuff, you'll never feel so awake. Lydden is a real contrast to that, tight and twisty with a top speed of 100mph, you need to grab hold of the car and man handle it round. Basically the race starts, you fight the car and track for fifteen minutes (if you're lucky) and the race ends. Despite being the slowest circuit we visit, it's probably the most physically and mentally draining.

With a car that wasn't yet fully to my liking I ended up using the right foot to steer the car as much as the steering wheel…I must have been getting more confident! Being inside a race car is always an aggressive and loud place to be but it seemed particularly loud on that day as I did my best to coax a laptime out of the car. As we left the circuit at the end of qualifying and queued up to be noise tested (Lydden is just about the only circuit to noise test cars after they've been on circuit, and no I don't understand it either) I spotted Dad stood a little further down holding one of our exhaust silencer inserts. Ah, it must have been VERY loud then.

A few minutes later and I was at the front of the cue and ready to be tested. I barely breathed on the throttle before I heard a definite 'FAIL' which came as no surprise. Fortunately Lydden is one of the more relaxed circuits with regards to noise levels and with a host of other very loud formulas on that day (sprint cars and the like) we were let off. I have the DVD of that meeting and no matter where my car is on the circuit you can hear it above everyone elses, sounding absolutely epic. Better put a new silencer on the list though, no way we're getting away with that racket anywhere else!

My efforts in qualifying had left me eighth on the nineteen car grid, prime territory for first lap shenanigans! As it happened it all kicked off right at the front of the grid at turn one this time though, which sent cars scattering in all directions. I've always done reasonably well when it comes to avoiding crashes (touch wood) and the gaps opened up nicely for me this time as I powered through into third position, game on! I was then met with the most annoying thing any race driver will see after making up a bunch of positions on the first lap, a red flag!

With a total restart and all the cars back in position we had another more successful attempt at the start (or less successful from my point of view as I wasn't running third this time) and a rather uneventful race to seventh position. Happily number seven was drawn out of the hat for pole position for race two, the Tigra had its first start from pole. Quick, change the set-up!

There's nothing better than being in the lead with a completely clear track in front of you (unless you happen to have a completely clear track behind you too) and it stayed that way for the first two laps before I was relegated to second place which became third on the next lap. With Lydden being so much narrower than the other circuits however, it is possible to defend and so despite not quite having the pace to clear off up the road, I did find myself still holding onto a podium spot into lap ten. A bit of a tussle behind had left only the dominant Matt Simpson close by and I didn't put up much of a fight, not wanting to risk dropping myself into the train of cars further back. As it turns out I wish I had though as Matt was carrying a bit of damage from earlier on in the race! Still, fourth place with the leader in sight was another step forward. With the increased grid sizes we even got a little trophy to put on the dashboard of the Transit on the way home and it had been a while since we could say that.

33 ARE WE FRONT RUNNERS YET?

A good result always gives you more motivation and so the list of improvements to be made before the next meeting was bigger than ever, not that you'd have known it. When we arrived at Snetterton the car looked much the same as it had at the previous meeting, but it was now sporting new lighter rear wings, sills and tailgate. We were still a little over our minimum weight of 850kgs (including driver) but we were getting closer. Coupled with the fact that I'd saved some new tyres for Snetterton, one of my favoured circuits, and I was hopeful of another good result.

The car felt great in qualifying and after a quick pitstop to have a loose door taped on (Motorsport – 1001 uses for duct tape) I could lap with some of the top guys, this could be a good weekend. I knew I'd have a couple of my earlier laps disallowed for running wide out of the final corner. In an effort to keep the drivers on the circuit, MSV had installed sensors in the areas just past the kerbs. (You'll also find them at Brands Hatch amongst others) If you run wide onto these sensors then a static camera automatically takes a photo that is immediately flashed up in race control, and there goes your laptime. Big brother is watching! Pretty clever stuff but you have to think that if most of the circuits didn't place inviting tarmac / concrete / grasscrete or astroturf etc past the kerbs then the drivers wouldn't be tempted out there in the first place. And if one person does it then everyone has to. Personally I'd do away with all tarmac runoffs, let's bring back an actual penalty for driving off the track, not a get out of jail free card. Watch some racing at a corner with a gravel trap and see how many drivers go off....

Back at Snetterton and with a couple good laptimes under my belt, and the end of the session drawing closer, it was time for one of my 'late banzai laps' as Dad calls them. I was lucky enough to win a very useful video camera and predictive laptimer system from Racelogic a few years previously that gives me laptime updates all the way round the circuit, a very useful tool and it was giving me lots of good news on my banzai lap at Snetterton. Every corner was perfect and every time I glanced at the dash it was reading another tenth under my previous best. By the time I was turning into the long Coram corner at the end of the lap I was seven tenths up on my previous best, the only problem was a huge gaggle of cars sat on the apex of the final corner who had all thought the session was over and were making their way back to the pits. Gutting!

Back in the pits I was delighted when I saw we were fourth on the grid and a little peeved to see that I could have had a front row if I'd been able to finish my fast lap. Argh! Still, good progress and all of a sudden the car was getting some much closer looks around the paddock.

Out on track I'd completely ballsed up the start of race one and dropped back to just outside the top ten. Although I had the pace to come back to sixth by the finish, it was clear that the car didn't have the ballistic pace it had had on new tyres in the morning. Clearly some more set-up work was required to make it all a bit kinder on the tyres. Despite this race two was much better and although I'd lost out to the ever rapid Simpson / Brockhurst duo in the first lap shuffle I managed to pick off the other cars starting front of me on the partially reversed grid to run in a clear third position after a few laps. The only fly in my ointment was Lewis Smith who came past and spent the rest of the race ever so gradually creeping away....much to my annoyance. If someone comes past you and disappears up the road then that's one thing, but when you can so nearly live with someone, but not quite, it's just infuriating. You're sweating your arse off in the car, trying to brake a few feet later, get on the power a few feet earlier, carry a couple extra mph through the apex, but no matter what you do the car in front is undeniably getting further up the road. Maddening. There's nothing like it to make you wish you'd spent a bit longer in the garage before the meeting, a bit longer trying to get some more weight out of the car…

Another fourth place then. Still a great result and I remember looking in my mirror as I crossed the line and seeing Malcolm Blackman battling with Simon Smith coming out of the last corner. Wow, we'd just driven away from them. That put a smile on our faces all the way home, as did our second 'egg cup trophy' of the season on the dashboard of the Transit.

After racing on the circuits for a few years by this point we had the excitement of a new circuit for the sixth round of 2014 in the shape of Donington Park. We'd been due to race at Donington in 2013 but the meeting had been cancelled as a result of the problems the circuit was having at the time with their proposed development to enable the hosting of Formula 1. Since then that has all fallen through of course and a great deal of time and money has been spent to put the whole place back to exactly how it was in the first place. Which is a good thing because it's amazing just the way it is.

There hadn't been so much excitement amongst the drivers on a track walk since our visit to Cadwell two years previous. Fingers crossed we weren't all ill this time though. As we strolled down the Craner curves in the evening sun, Dad used his pushbike to demonstrate just how steep it really was by disappearing off down the hill at some knots. Needless to say he took considerably longer to get up the other side. By the time we'd walked to the bottom of the hill and had a good long look at the famous wall on the outside of the Old Hairpin, which Nigel Mansell spectacularly collected in a Touring Car in 1999, we knew we were in for some fun the following day. Simon announced that he thought the Old Hairpin would be taken flat out, I made a mental note to stay out of his way in qualifying!

Come race day and hopes were high of another strong meeting, but I just wasn't feeling comfortable during my first few laps of the circuit. After finding myself a bit of clear air and giving myself a bit of a talking to, I started trying to put a quick lap together. No sooner had I thought this and I felt the engine tighten up as I powered out of a corner before dying completely. Well ****! Gauges look okay and there's no smoke, oil, water or fire anywhere, but that definitely felt like a dying engine. Bump across the grass and park up at a marshals post. After watching everyone else finish the session and getting a tow back to the pits we finally got to have a proper nose at the car to see what had gone wrong. "No sign of anything amiss under the bonnet, flick the ignition on a minute" A flick of the switch and no sign of life. Strange. "Ah! I know!" It turns out the lambda sensor we'd fitted for the meeting had blown a fuse. This wouldn't have been a problem except that it had been wired through the ignition so it had taken that with it too. I'd accidently twisted the wires when fitting the sensor and they'd shorted out, whoops! Who let the postman do the electrics? At least it was an easy fix and the car was fighting fit for race one. What had felt like the engine 'tightening up' was just the feeling of massive compression when the fuse blew and turned it off.

It's always interesting being in a race when you don't have any idea of braking points or what gear to be in for which corner, but that's just what you have to deal with sometimes. It has to be said the car felt fantastic and once I started to figure the circuit out a little I could make massive ground on the cars ahead at every corner. I was making up places and eyeing up some of the more 'upper midfield runners' further ahead thinking I could still have a crack at them later on in the race. I missed a gear coming out of the chicane as I tried to cut under another car and the engine screamed in protest before I had another stab at third gear. Another scream from the engine. That could be another problem then. A gentle attempt at getting on the throttle in fourth gear sent the car slewing across the track. Ah, halfshaft then. Not fancying crawling round a full lap with one wheel drive I pulled off down the Craners and met some more lovely marshals. As nice as they were I'd have much rather been in the race!

Back in the pits we had to very rapidly swap the halfshaft and diff over before race two as the broken end of halfshaft had well and truly wedged itself in the diff. This also means removing the undertray, rear wing, and tailgate, all on a day where only me and Dad were present and the meeting timetable seemed to be cruelly tight. We managed it but there wasn't a great deal of time to spare, just about enough for the obligatory nervous pre-race pee. (Vitally important part of racing!)

Not finishing race one meant starting race two from the back. It's always depressing when you look in your mirror on the warm-up lap and see nothing besides the medical car, but on the bright side the only way is forwards! The car wasn't quite as good as in the first race as our spare diff was set differently, but it wasn't bad and I was making steady if unspectacular progress through the order.

By mid race I was enjoying being in a great four car tussle for fifth place. It's hard work being involved in the middle of a group but good fun also. The actual task of driving the car has to go into 'automatic mode' while you're busy trying to figure out how to get past the car in front. Is he struggling anywhere? Am I strong at any of those points? Can I get him to defend somewhere to get him off-line so I can have a go at the next corner? Some of the best overtaking moves are set-up half a lap in advance! Of course whilst all this is going on there's someone else behind you trying to do exactly the same thing. It's like a high speed game of chess. Even when a line of cars seem to be holding static positions for lap after lap, all this is still going on, with each driver trying to outwit the others. The better you know the drivers you're racing with, the better you can predict the outcome too. There are times you'll see a couple of the more, shall we say 'lively' drivers doing battle in front, and on those occasions it can be better to hang back and wait for the inevitable to happen, picking up the pieces when it does. There's certainly a lot of thinking going on inside the crash helmets.

Back at Donington and I was struggling to make any impression on the cars in front of me so I was hoping for something to kick off, which it did, allowing me to sneak past into fifth as the other cars bounced through the gravel trap at the chicane.

Donington was one of those meetings where you find yourself travelling home afterwards and wishing you could have another go at it. It's certainly a fun circuit to drive and without the problems it could have been one of our best meetings of the year. But there's a lot of could haves, if's and buts in motorsport! At the end of the day you've just got to do the best you can with the cards you're dealt. Anyone can be good on the odd day everything falls for them, but most of the time you've got to work a bit to make things go your way.

34 WELL THAT WENT QUICKLY

With the season fast approaching its end we had another visit to Lydden Hill in place of our originally scheduled Silverstone visit. Even this late in the season and we'd made some changes to the car with the addition of some residual pressure valves in the brake lines and extra winglets and fins at the front and rear of the car. I'm fascinated by aerodynamics and if you check the bookmarks on my laptop you'll find a whole host of articles covering everything from wings and splitters to cooling and flow separation. Then there's a massive stack of Racecar Engineering magazines with post it notes highlighting interesting info. There are of course many more post-its and bookmarks highlighting useful set-up information and driving articles, in fact if I remembered everything I read I could probably give Adrian Newey a run for his money! Unfortunately that isn't the case but you've got to try! Even if the extra aero didn't work, it did at least make the car look like the Batmobile, which must be a good thing surely?

Despite all the work I only managed a disappointing tenth on the grid. Even though the car had gotten better during the year, we had definitely found a few problems which would need to be rectified over the winter break. That's the thing about race cars, they're never really finished.

Being in the midfield at Lydden Hill on lap one is very much like being in a short oval race, lots of cars and not much track! I hadn't had the best opening few corners and was looking like going backwards more than forwards. As the pack flew up the hill towards the hairpin there was the inevitable bunching of cars on the inside so I decided to throw it down the outside. Well, I was so far back there wasn't much to lose! Braking late and I found myself alongside Simon Smith in the middle of the hairpin. I seemed to always be somewhere near him over the second half of the season and that's quite a good thing because he's a very fast fair driver to race with. The previous year it had been Mark Fuller who'd always been in close proximity and we'd enjoyed some cracking races, days when you get out of the car and it doesn't really matter where you've finished, you've just had a bloody good race.

Back at Lydden and I came out of the hairpin on the outside of Simon. To make things more interesting, Lewis Smith had nosed up the inside of Simon coming off the corner so as we accelerated down the appropriately named 'Hairy Hill' towards the equally scary Paddock bend, I was the third car out, and that's not a good place to be. With so many cars close behind, backing out of it didn't look like a good idea, and I had a touch of momentum, so I stayed wide, gritted my teeth (vitally important) and turned in. I thought it might all end in a crash, and I wouldn't have been mad if it had, but I got away with it and just about had enough track to play with as the back end drifted out and tickled the gravel trap on the exit. Sixth place, that's more like it!

With the end of race one in sight, light rain began falling. Not enough to affect the circuit and my progress to fifth place, but as soon as we were back in the paddock the heavens really opened. Drivers and teams abandoned cars and ran for cover as the rain bounced off the tarmac, race two really would be interesting.

This would be the first time I'd driven the Tigra in the wet and although we were given two warming up laps to get a feel for the atrocious conditions, they were run at about 30mph, which was just about fast enough to tell that going anywhere near the throttle pedal was going to cause problems. Undeterred the safety car pulled off and we went racing. As soon as the pack of cars ahead accelerated out of the final corner, the spray intensified and visibility dropped.

Pick a braking point for turn one based on experience and instinct, that was okay. Fight the back end coming off the corner and power round the outside of one of the front row starting cars to take fourth. The quick boys won't be far behind, make the moves now and bugger off into the distance while they squabble in the mist. Brake hard for the next left and feel the car rise and fall over a river crossing the track, there's one to avoid next lap.

No sooner had I thought things were going well and the windscreen wiper stopped working. No! A frantic flick of the switch does nothing and attention focuses back to the race as there's a hairpin looming. I've got the back end dancing in all directions as I'm too impatient with the throttle on the exit, but everything's still pointing in the right direction and I'm up to third. A few more irate flicks of the switch and the wiper still stubbornly refuses to cooperate as I head onto lap two, can I drive like this?

There's only two cars ahead but even they're throwing enough water at me to make things difficult. At least the screen hasn't steamed up at all and I can still make out the edges of the track. As long as I don't get too close to anything I reason it's just about bearable, even if it's mightily annoying as the car feels good and I'm pretty sure I could be hunting down the leaders if I could see!

A few laps later and I lose a position to Simon Smith who was flying along and set the fastest lap of the race. I had to give up a bit of distance to him for the sake of visibility but I was pleased to move back into third a few laps later as Jason Hunn slid wide. The race seemed to be going on forever as I put a lap on my old car which looked like a handful in the conditions, I could empathise, I knew what that car was like at this track in the wet!

Lap after lap, surely this race must be nearly over? I could just about make out Matt Simpson and Malcolm Blackman in my mirrors, slowly reeling me in. It's a bit like a death sentence seeing that pairing of double Intermarque champion and double National Hotrod World Champion catching you up, you'd rather you were being pursued by Lord Voldemort. I tried to push a little harder and had a bit of a moment as I caught a big puddle I couldn't see.

Conditions definitely getting worse then, mental note to stay off that piece of track.

There were a few dicey moments as we dived through the backmarkers which was to be expected as we could barely see each other through the spray. Still the order remained the same until Matt relegated me to fourth as we entered the last lap with Malcolm following through soon after as I struggled to see in Matts wake. I had half an idea of trying a move back at the last turn but as we built up speed towards the corner, the combined spray of the two cars ahead, and another backmarker, was like standing under a waterfall and looking up. Another fifth then. Pleasing in the circumstances but would this outright podium ever come?

After giving everything a good airing following the Lydden Hill soaking, we began preparing for the final meeting of the year where we would be a supporting formula at the Brands Hatch British Truck meeting. I've never understood the fascination of racing trucks, but maybe that's because we have to race after they've been out on circuit and covered it in that wonderful combination of water and diesel. I know they draw a crowd but I'd be far happier to see them clogging up some motorway instead of demolishing the circuits. Be that as it may, we were of course at Brands Hatch where the Intermarques managed their best grid of the season with 23 competitive cars, all competing in the one class. Amazing progress over the previous few seasons and with so many more potential drivers milling around the paddock it looks like being a bright future for the championship, move over BTCC!

The thought of a race meeting in early November is always cause for concern, especially to those of us who camp, but aside from a brief shower on raceday morning, it was fantastic all weekend. The brief shower did occur during qualifying however which certainly livened up proceedings! A little bit of rain when you've got hot tyres isn't so much of an issue, but cold slicks, light rain and a greasy track is an eye opening experience as the car squirms under you. With the rain stopping you have to constantly re-evaluate how much grip you have and by the end of the session we were down to dry lap times.

With the advent of modern technology, anyone with an internet connection and a computer or a smartphone can follow the live timings for pretty much any motor racing event in the UK at real time. It's so good that Dangerous Tim often knows the results before we do, and he's sat on his sofa hundreds of miles away! On this particular occasion the smartphones were out and following the qualifying session live at the circuit. After running around the fringes of the top ten for most of the session it was looking like being a mid-grid start. "No, no, no" said Dad when shown the live timings "we haven't had his banzai laps at the end yet" He does know me well.

Banzai laps completed and fifth place on the most competitive grid of the year was a morale boosting start to the day. As we lined up in the assembly area for race one it really struck me how much we'd improved over the previous seasons. You're always so engrossed in the next development or working your way into the next group of drivers that you don't notice the gradual upturn in performance, and that others are now working towards being able to race with you. It's a nice thought.

I fumbled the start of race one by cracking into the rev limiter off the rolling start which will always cost you a car length or two. Slightly miffed at myself I dived into Paddock, stubbornly following the rapid Chris Brockhurst ahead of me. I've always admired Chris' driving and hoped that we're on a similar journey results wise, just that I'm a couple seasons behind him!

The entry speed into Paddock from a tight inside line on lap one suddenly felt too fast, and as if to confirm that thought, Chris' car swapped ends on him as he braked behind Blackman. I was moments behind him as the rear end of my car also snapped away. I hastily wound on all the opposite lock I had, although in truth with Chris' sideways car taking up most of the track in front of me, and me currently staring at the infield, there was almost a resigned acceptance of the fact that we were going to spin and be collected by the twenty or so cars behind. Not the way to end the season! Miraculously, and I suspect with some luck involved, I got the car straightened up just in time to dodge Chris and speed away towards

Druids in third place. It was one of those 'Did I really just get away with that?' moments.

Not everyone had gotten off so luckily and the safety car was out for a few laps while a handful of mangled cars were dragged clear. I spent those laps trying to feel if everything was okay with the car. I was almost certain it was but a small nagging part of my brain was telling me that slide at turn one had been caused by a fault somewhere, or oil leaking onto a tyre, or one of the other million and one things that can go wrong with a race car. I also knew I was in third place and no disrespect to Mike Thurley behind me, who is a good driver, but I thought I had the measure of him that day. I just hoped he started fighting with those lined up behind him!

With the race back underway I was a bit steady for the first few turns while I convinced myself all was well with the car, but then I was off and opened up a gap to the cars behind. Simpson and Blackman had cleared off up the road in their dispute over the win but third would do me nicely. Despite having clear track I wasn't quite managing to get the laptimes I was after though and to make things worse the rapid Lewis Smith and Simon Smith were soon into fourth and fifth.

A desperate attempt to keep them at arms length only resulted in cooked brakes and cooked rear tyres which made it fairly easy for them to come past with four minutes of the race remaining, as shown on that awful Brands Hatch countdown clock.

Another fifth place at the flag then, a result to be proud of in such a big field but just a little frustrating. Fifth place had seemed to be our position for most of the second half of the season, we were even fifth in the championship, although that position would still be up for grabs in the second race of the day, the last of the season.

After the excitement of turn one in race one, I was much more cautious in race two. Sometimes being cautious in a race car is a bad thing and as a result of all the caution at turn one I got passed into turn one, out of turn one and then most of the way around the first lap until I was down to tenth. It's a mark of how much racier the championship is getting that once you're on the backfoot it's very easy to lose a whole host of places. I'm pleased to say I bounced back to sixth a few laps later, and whilst making sure I kept Ray Harris at arms length, and trying to reel in Keith White and Simon Smith ahead, I was also doing some maths and figuring out that the current results would be enough for me to maintain fifth in the championship by a mere three points. Just don't make a mistake!

If I'd had maybe an hour I could have caught the two cars ahead, but in truth the car was getting more and more difficult to drive, my arms were killing me, my leg was burning on the gearbox tunnel and Ray was nearly getting into striking range behind me, so I was happy to see the chequered flag.

Sixth place in the race and fifth place in the championship. Best of the rest, behind the 'big four' of Matt Simpson, Malcolm Blackman, Chris Brockhurst and Lewis Smith. Not a bad effort seeing we'd started the season with a brand new, completely home built and untested car, driven by a postman. We were pretty proud of that. As our friend Tony said about the car, 'designed by two lunatics and built in a shed'. Fairly accurate.

On the way home from that final meeting of 2014, Mum asked what was happening the following Sunday. "Working on the car of course, lots of changes to make over the winter…" Of course, she knew that's what we were going to say.

That's the fantastic thing about all levels of motorsport, there's always just one more season.

ABOUT THE AUTHOR

Ross Loram is a self-confessed motorsport addict. If he's not racing, then the chances are he's at work earning some money to go racing. Or at the garage working on the race car. You can follow his adventures at www.loramracing.co.uk

Printed in Germany
by Amazon Distribution
GmbH, Leipzig